NOTES ON LIVING UNTIL WE SAY GOODBYE

A Personal Guide

NOTES ON LIVING UNTIL WE SAY GOODBYE

A Personal Guide

LON G. NUNGESSER
WITH
WILLIAM D. BULLOCK

ST. MARTIN'S PRESS
NEW YORK

155.9

LIBRARY OF CONGRESS
Library of Congress Cataloging-in-Publication Data

Nungesser, Lon G.
  Notes on living until we say goodbye : a personal guide / by
Lon Nungesser.
    p.   cm.
  ISBN 0-312-01517-8 : $14.95
  1. Death—Psychological aspects. 2. Terminally ill—
Psychology.   I. Title
BF789.D4N86   1988
155.9'—dc19   87-27474
                                                            CIP

First Edition

10 9 8 7 6 5 4 3 2 1

To my parents
for teaching me that you don't have to understand
in order to care.

CONTENTS

Contents

ACKNOWLEDGMENTS

I want to thank each and every person "living with dying" with whom I was in contact during the experience of writing this book. I am particularly grateful to the members of the team who worked on this book with me. I want to thank Lois Smith for her careful review and insightful comments. Thanks to Diane Roberts and her family for encouragement while I coped with the obstacles in my journey of "living with writing this book." I thank my editor, Michael Denneny, for his direction, discipline, and most of all for believing in me. Special thanks to Dr. Peter Lucy for his "steadfastness at the helm" while I wrote this book.

PREFACE

In this book I combine practical information gleaned from the professional and technical literature on illness and death with knowledge gained by my own life-promoting and life-threatening experiences. I deal with the issues and events that come up for people facing a life-threatening illness in the order they generally occur: from diagnosis to empowerment, through stigma and daily coping, to hope and denial, and on to savoring the past and being still alive.

This book focuses on individual self-determination, on freedom in medical decision-making. *Notes on Living Until We Say Goodbye* aims to help the individual to create medical situations in which the physician is the patient's ally. This book is based on a humanist view that fosters the right to reject, disagree with, or work with persons who have medical authority. It emphasizes the advantages of having an open awareness of one's mortality and an active involvement in promoting one's health. But it teaches each of us to do more than exist with illness by emphasizing survival with a bit of the good life.

Etched in the heart of this book is this motto:

"It is your life. Live it now!"

NOTE TO THE READER

I wrote this book to other young and middle-age people who have been told they have a terminal illness. I hope it will also benefit our friends, family members, and care providers. I wanted to explore the concerns that surround and sometimes bombard us, from the impact of diagnosis to finding yourself still alive afterward. I wrote this book because I believe that as long as we are still alive, we should continue to learn and share; here I ask you to explore many of the important issues and events you'll likely come up against in the course of living with dying. The discussion is based on an appreciation of death in the evolution of civilized mortals, "those who die."

Notes on Living Until We Say Goodbye

A Personal Guide

ONE

TERMINAL DIAGNOSIS:

From Dread to Empowerment

This is some way to spend my lunch hour, I thought as I loosened my blue wool tie. I gently placed my right hand over the five-day-old biopsy incision on my left forearm. I closed my eyes for a moment and sighed deeply, saying a few reassuring words to myself. I had made it through some incredible events before. I had never been very ill, though. I had always taken my health for granted. But today I dreaded hearing what the doctor might say was wrong with me.

I had been sitting in the dermatology waiting room for nearly an hour. My eyes shifted from the pale blue walls to the myriad of magazines on the table in front of me, as my mind drifted to my two-week-old job as Foreign Student Advisor for Stanford University. It was a fantastic career opportunity! I had so many exciting plans for the upcoming academic year.

My empty stomach was growling. I felt nervous and

1

unprepared. At last, the nurse came to escort me to the examination room. I anticipated a certain relief at hearing the answer to the question that had haunted me since the biopsy: "Am I going to die?" I followed the nurse apprehensively. The bottom of my shoes squeaked along the shiny linoleum floor in the hospital corridor.

Looking at my chart as she walked ahead of me, the nurse softly inquired, "Do you think you could arrange to take the afternoon off work?"

I told her that I could take off work, but I had not planned to. Sitting on the exam table, I asked her, "Will I need to?" I began rolling up my shirt sleeve and prepared for my "vitals" to be routinely taken. They were not. This lady in white was already on her way out the door! She replied quickly over her shoulder, "The doctor will be right in to talk with you."

Left alone in the sterile examination room, I pondered the meaning of her question. I wondered if I looked like a cancer patient. I looked at my watch as I thought, "In just a few minutes, I will know if these tiny spots on my skin are cancer." The days since biopsy had seemed so long, and the nights filled with dreadful anticipation. Nothing could be more off-time in my life than to die now! "Never trust anyone over thirty," was something I only recently had to stop saying.

The somber dermatologist began, "Mr. Nungesser, I'm afraid the results of the biopsy were positive for Kaposi's sarcoma cancer." In the next few seconds, I learned that I had a few months to live. This was not simply a life-threatening illness; I had a terminal cancer for which there was no cure.

Like the opening bars of Beethoven's Fifth Symphony, the doctor's confirmation of my diagnosis brought on a whirlwind of emotions. The doctor revealed that he could do little or nothing to save my life and, in this way, the negative impact of the diagnosis was greatly heightened.

I was shattered. I felt such intense loss. I feared dying with an empty feeling some place deep inside myself, where others have decades to fill. My immediate reaction to the news left me feeling vulnerable, caught unsheltered between the hammer and the anvil. I doubted that I would ever fulfill any of my life's goals and desires.

I actually accepted everything the diagnosing physician said about my chances for survival. I felt saturated in the fatalism of death emanating from the powerful authority of a medical doctor. There was no room for hope in this inn of doom and gloom.

Negative attitudes overshadowed my diagnosis, causing the diagnosis itself to be as negative an event as my illness. The illness was described as terminal, and the mental effect of that message was fatalism: I had received a *terminal diagnosis*.

First, I cried alone. I just sat in my car sobbing. It was the hospital parking lot, and no one even noticed. I just couldn't believe it. I had only started pursuing my career, and had been in a good relationship for two years. I was battered by extreme feelings: shock, chaos, anger, sadness, hopelessness, fear, and disbelief.

Then I prayed with a minister. I prayed to the God with whom I had long ago sought and found peace. I had been a pastor at the early age of seventeen, and I had been helping others deal with death and dying for a long time. My God represented all of my values and relationships, and was not a punitive God. I sought to find a spiritual challenge in my medical crisis: After all, I thought, it was not life that mattered, but the courage I brought to it. I wondered how I might accept this challenge, and searched my mind for reasons to do so. After I had cried for about an hour in church, I dried my eyes and looked up to the colorful rays of sunlight shining through stained glass windows. I took a few deep breaths. I stood up, and walked into the bright afternoon sun. I was grateful that I could feel the crisp autumn air blowing on my face.

I felt the need to talk with someone, but not someone I was concerned about having to take care of. So, I sought out a trusted friend to help me begin getting a grip on this news. Looking back, it seems like I was in a haze, guided along by an intense and unfamiliar desire to survive. Fortunately, I followed my gut re-action and talked with someone who was responsive. As the first person to hear the news, this woman had a lot of influence on how I reacted to my diagnosis. Two of the most important things my friend did were to accept my emotional reactions without judging me,

2. and to tell me how others had coped well with similar medical crises. She seemed to stay composed, yet she was obviously concerned.] I don't remember what I said; I rambled on in shock. Three years later, my friend (a counselor) revealed to me how utterly helpless she had felt when I told her of my diagnosis. She said she believed that I could and should find my own way to deal with having cancer. She reminded me that I had already coped with tough times and succeeded. She gave me several resources to consider for a wide range of services. Her approach to alternative health care was made clear by her referrals. In fact, this person had been taught by her parents that one's health is in one's control. The social services she referred me to did not have services for people with AIDS, but the spirit they were given in helped. It opened my eyes to a wide range of choices in both how I saw my illness and how I might deal with it.

Her comforting approach and thoughtfulness gave me the feeling of being cared for and capable. I felt okay about my need to be connected to others in a mutually supportive way. With her compassionate encouragement, I found my self-reliance.

A lot of the initial impact of my AIDS diagnosis was due to the stigma of this new disease. After an AIDS diagnosis, it is common for a patient to assume he or she will die in a few months, and health care professionals have reported numerous cases in which the patient does not even ask about his prognosis. These patients have heard the media screams of how deadly

AIDS is. They don't need to be told again, especially when it is they who have the disease. Unfortunately, this kind of "Why bother?" attitude toward their own health sends many people to an isolated room where they listen to the clock tick away as they await an early grave.

Author and cancer patient Natalie D. Spingarn writes, "What is said to the patient at the time a diagnosis is made is particularly important. It sets the stage, as it were, for how the patient and his or her family deal with the disease from then on."

Within a week after my diagnosis, the dermatologist referred me to an oncologist. The oncologist said I might live for as much as two years, and she would make me as comfortable as possible. This cancer specialist encouraged me to begin systemic chemotherapy. I asked for another referral.

This time I went to an internal medicine doctor with some experience in dealing with Kaposi's sarcoma cancer. He urged me to be a candidate for a new experimental protocol to begin the following month at a West Coast teaching hospital. I protested the use of experimental immunosuppressive treatments, because I had observed that they often preceded the onset of serious infections that are generally known to result from a declining immunity. It simply made no sense to me to undertake treatment that would worsen my primary immune disorder. The internal medicine doctor shot back, "What have you got to lose?"

As I got up to leave his office for the first and last time, I replied, "My life. And what have I to gain?"

"A chance at survival," he said.

Suddenly learning that you have a life-threatening illness is like having the floor drop right out from under you. I have found that one of my first steps in surviving diagnosis was to acknowledge and accept some of the beliefs, emotions, and desires swirling through me that were unfamiliar and difficult. Some recently diagnosed people feel emotionally paralyzed by shame and guilt. One man I talked with said that after receiving a terminal cancer diagnosis he "did not hear anything the doctor said . . . I left the doctor's office in a stupor."

Your age will have something to do with how you react to a terminal diagnosis. The meaning you ascribe to such a death sentence will be guided by your own expectations for living. Old people are commonly thought to die gracefully, as children pass on gently. Because of my own circumstance, I am decidedly focusing on the experiences of young adults and middle-aged persons with terminal illnesses.

Your initial reactions can make the difference between taking charge of your living and giving in to dying. Try to keep in mind the importance of gaining a clear understanding of what is happening to you. Now you know a very important fact: Your diagnosis has been confirmed. There will be many other medical and social facts emerging about your illness, but once you have integrated this basic news into your life you

can begin to build confidence in the specifics of what
to do and how to do it. Your goal through the days
immediately after receiving a terminal diagnosis should
be to take steps to govern your well-being. You will
gradually learn ways to handle one day at a time, "to
paddle your own canoe."

You may need a person or several people to talk with
in order to get a handle on this event. There may be
a lot of people you will have to tell. You may even
have to face some of them on the job right after your
doctor's appointment, or at home later. Many of the
decisions you will have to make now about disclosing
your diagnosis will appear again and again as you cope
with other physical events and social changes.

But you should be especially careful about the *first*
person you tell about your illness, for this person's
beliefs about your illness can influence you. Some people might give up on you, feeling you are not worth
the energy that caring would require. These people
will split when the going gets tough, and defend their
inability to cope by irrational anger toward you. Many
people will begin to see you as needy and helpless.
Some people will become cold and defensive. Some
people will have their own way of "falling off the wagon
of your life." Others will lend you a helping hand,
listening to what you need. Still others will comfort
you as you grow to handle your situation.

You will need to decide in each case how to deal
with telling people about your medical news. Depending on what led you to be diagnosed and how you

were told, you will have some choices about whom you choose to tell and how you decide to tell them.

Here are some questions to consider when you are deciding who should be the first person you confide in:

- How comfortable do you feel when you are in that person's company?

- Could this person handle the news without needing so much that their own need adds to your burden?

- Can the person realistically keep your secret for the period of time you may want?

- How confident is this person in your ability to deal with crises?

- Are they the type to encourage you not to give up?

- Are they the kind of person who can help both you and the other people you will want to tell?

Your life after diagnosis will lead you to tell particular people at the right times. You probably won't—and shouldn't—tell everyone at once. It may help to space your disclosures out over a few days or weeks, telling the people closest to you first, and selected friends later. You won't want to tell everyone in your life about it.

The limits and requirements you have about whom to tell and when to tell them should be thought through until you are clear about them. Don't forget to ask yourself why you think you should tell someone of your news. Take the time to create a special way to tell them, one that respects the feelings between you.

How you tell someone can make a big difference in the way that person will treat you. For example, if you say, "I'm dying," you might encourage an atmosphere of helplessness. In contrast, if you say, "Such-and-such a test reports that I have a life-threatening illness," you might leave some room for positive hope. How you tell someone should be clearly based on how much information you feel comfortable giving them. Think about how much is necessary. Think about how much is desirable. Consider how each person may react. Weigh the benefits of telling them against the damages of not telling them.

A critical aspect involved in being at the helm of your life right after receiving a terminal diagnosis is dealing with self-blame. It was one of the first things I had to come to terms with after my diagnosis. I wondered hour after hour, "Why did it have to be me?" I found comfort in knowing that bad things *do* happen to good people. I replied to the "Why me?" question with "Why anyone?" This enabled me to see the obvious: All things in life are not fair; we do not always deserve what we get.

I resolved that I would do all I could to take responsibility for managing my health and well-being *one day at a time.* If I couldn't do anything about a problem today, I tried to put it out of my mind. I concentrated on solving the problems here and now, realizing that every day could be lived as though it was my last. It made life easier for me to handle the day at hand, less overwhelming. I took responsibility for my past, while leaving blame and shame behind me.

Whenever my mind would wander back to questions about what I did to deserve this illness, I'd say: *Don't dwell.* In fact, sometimes I yelled it.

I was inspired to continue this approach by a book by Jaffe, Rudin, and Rudin entitled, *Why Me? Why Anyone?* (New York: St. Martin's Press, 1986). This book contains the story of a courageous rabbi and his remarkable struggle with life-threatening illness. It deals with the issues of religion and guidance, friendship, and human suffering.

Another central feature of conducting your life after a terminal diagnosis is dealing with feelings. These feelings may be of a new intensity and of a confusing variety. Communicating these feelings to other people will present new social challenges for you.

As you travel further down the path of facing a life-threatening illness, beyond the dread of diagnosis to your empowerment, you sometimes won't really believe you are strong enough to be brave, and that's okay, too. Remember it's the unyielding oak that breaks in the wind, and the graceful, flexible willow that bends with it. And like the willow tree, you will need to weep as you endure the whip of this stormy wind. As a person with a life-threatening illness, you may have to spend a lot of effort managing the quality of your emotional life. Achieving emotional clarity amidst a chaos of feelings is not an easy task. You can't count on having one clear emotional state at a time. There may be times when you just don't know what the heck you are feeling.

When you are feeling overwhelmed or confused, it helps to write out your feelings. When I sorted out my feelings about the things happening to me and around me, I used 3 × 5 cards and I wrote an emotion on each card. For example, I wrote sadness on one card, happy on another, and so forth. The first time I did this exercise, I must have listed forty emotions, including: nervous, loneliness, bitterness, hatred, confusion, hurt, emptiness, frustration, humiliation, peacefulness, envy, overwhelmed, powerful, out of control, blah, satisfied, and scared.

I first sorted the Emotion-cards in stacks based on how similar each was to the others. My Anger card was right on top of my Sadness card, and my Happy card was close to my Worthwhile card. Clearly, my anger and sadness were somehow related to one another. But I didn't know why. So I also wrote the name of each important person in my life on another set of 3 × 5 cards. Then I re-sorted the cards with my feelings on them, placing Emotion-cards on People-cards; this revealed some interesting contradictions between my feelings about the people on the cards. Some relationships were characterized by harmonious emotions, others were made of conflict. I discovered that I was acting satisfied toward some people with whom I was really unhappy.

I made Event-cards on another occasion, to depict the significant things that were happening in my life. For instance, I listed my diagnosis on one card, losing my job on another, having a friend whose illness was getting worse on one, and having friends abandon me in my time of need on another card. Then, I sorted my Feeling-cards on to the Event-cards. This revealed some of the specific feelings generated by specific events. Being diagnosed made me feel angry and sad, as did being abandoned by my friends. I saw more clearly how I was reacting to my illness and to others' reactions to my illness. There were a lot of reasons for me to be upset in these various ways. I clarified my values about living by examining the feelings certain people and events evoked in me. I grew to understand that I wouldn't be feeling these things if I didn't value consistent friendship and honest communication. This exercise led me to think of ways to gain satisfaction in my life. I became more aware of the times when my feelings were letting me know it was time to change my expectations toward others and when it was time to do something constructive about a major life event.

Having a life-threatening illness can be intense; death always seems to lurk nearby. It is important that we nurture in ourselves a simultaneous denial *and* acceptance of dying. There is something very freeing about realizing how mortal each of us is. Beyond the acceptance of mortality awaits choice. For example, it is possible to accept that one has a limited time to live and deny that fact the power to influence negatively your choices about how you spend that time. The bottom line is that you deserve to be happy and you are worth whatever it takes to enjoy today, as you set and pursue valuable goals.

You may need to rely on others in new and different ways. Be open and frank in ongoing discussions with the people you trust. When you feel that someone you care for has hurt you, tell them what you felt after the upsetting incident. When close friends disappoint you, express your disappointment. By talking openly about your anger and your disappointment with another, you will learn about your expectations and your desires. If anger and disappointment are not familiar terrain to you and your friend, then admitting this newness together can actually reaffirm your friendship.

One of your greatest tasks will be to live by your personal appreciation of how imperfect and mortal each one of us really is. Yet if you are able to forgive others, it can help you to forgive yourself for having difficulties or making errors. The act of forgiveness is actually secondary to your overall awareness of our mortality and imperfection. You don't have to let go of all standards for intimacy; on the contrary, sometimes you will have to define your values by rejecting some potential friendships and accepting others.

The key to creating satisfaction with your life is in this open and direct manner of communicating with others. Focus on what you can do, not what you used to be able to do. Select your social network carefully now. In doing so, you are increasing the chances that the period of time you have before you can be one of comfort and satisfaction.

Still, facing death is a fearsome and difficult fact of life for most people. Death is typically shown on television and in films as violent and abrupt. Sometimes it is romanticized. Because of this "pornography of death" the common reactions of others may include a fading fascination followed by intense anxiety and dreadful anticipations. We are quick to sense that, while it may take only a few seconds to die, there is an inherent horror that arises from living with the dread of death.

It is no surprise that the intensity of familiar emotions may make them unrecognizable. I've never felt such intense emotions as those that facing death stirs in me. I believe it helps me to remember that these intense feelings represent an appropriate reaction to this life-threatening event.

Some feelings are more easily acknowledged than others. We are more familiar with emotions like affection or attraction than bone-chilling terror. Part of the reason for various degrees of familiarity with an emotion is how often an emotion has moved you in your life. Some feelings, like sadness, occur with relative frequency. Other feelings, like quaking fear of impending doom, may never have been a part of your experience, or, at least, not often.

Talking with others who are going through what you are can help you to learn about these unfamiliar feelings. Right after I was diagnosed, for example, I had the unfamiliar feeling of doubting that I could rely on my own body. I had always been a very self-reliant individual. I could always count on myself. It helped me to talk to other young men who were like me, and recently diagnosed with AIDS. These feelings I was having of fearing the loss of biological self-control were also common among the others, as were the emotions of fear, anger, and dread that the situation created in each of us.

I have experienced what some people would call psychological phases, during which I would go from confronting the illness head-on to getting away from thinking about it. I have discovered that it is healthy to strike a balance between actively coping and simply being here now.

Don't let yourself get into a rut that reflects either an "I don't deserve to be happy," or an "I shouldn't be happy, people will think I'm nuts" attitude. You do deserve to be satisfied with life's special moments of pleasure. The most evil denial is not to deny death, but to deny life.

You may also find it helpful to simply distract yourself sometimes with a healthy activity you enjoy, like watching a movie. You've got to give yourself some relief, in fact, you've got to *plan* to give yourself some time and activities that bring you relief. Reading is often a rewarding activity. Being outside in a park can be a treat. Going to the masseur is nice. Activities that make one laugh, like funny films and games, jokes and cartoons, give a healthy break from the daily hassles and crises brought about by your illness.

Taking charge of your medical treatment is another necessary part of moving from dread to empowerment. My decision to remain active and to cope with living and dying in the first few months after my diagnosis led me to confront some major health decisions. If I felt that a health event demanded a medical or social decision that was impossible for me to make because I lacked the information to do so, I sought the necessary knowledge. Demanding more information in order to make well-informed medical decisions is a good idea. And, as important, the act of information gathering encourages a strong will to actively participate in one's survival.

A lot of other people are involved in this search to take charge of one's own health care. The *Wall Street Journal* (April 24, 1987, page 1) printed a special issue dedicated to this "consumer movement." Author William E. Blundell argued that, "One of the most stunning—and frequently overlooked—developments in medicine today is the sea of change occurring in patients' attitudes. Essentially, patients are in revolt against the doctors and other elements of the health care system that have patronized them, kept them in the dark and treated them either as objects or as children expected to passively obey."

Cancer consultants agree that some of us are required

to make incredibly important decisions immediately, without the knowledge of what's right. "Not knowing" was the worst part of the postdiagnosis period of my life. During the days right after diagnosis, the medical decisions I had to make caused me intense frustration because I didn't know what treatments would work best for my illness, which blood tests were most important and why they were important, and how much physical care I would need to plan for.

Many people recently diagnosed with terminal illness report feeling pressured to make decisions sooner than they are ready. I suggest talking with someone knowledgeable about several treatment options, a specialist or a person who has already gone past the same postdiagnosis shock. If possible, don't make decisions about what treatments you'll choose immediately. Take time to think it over. It is *your* decision. Taking some time to weigh your treatment alternatives usually won't threaten your longevity or make your immediate situation more critical. Take care not to let the incredible event of your diagnosis cast a cloud of urgency over you that impairs your ability to make sound medical decisions.

Make a mental note—or better still, a written one —about how the doctor put the decision to you, in terms of your survival with and without a particular treatment. Are you being given a choice between treatment now and treatment later, or between several genuine treatment alternatives? Be wary of occasions when the outcome of a treatment is put in life-or-death terms.

You may be influenced to try an experimental treatment if you are convinced that you have nothing to lose. Good information can be your first line of defense against these implications of your illness. You will enable yourself to fight for recovery, improving the quality of your life.

I have done several library searches on topics of interest to my own cancer and situation. I strongly recommend using your public library as a health resource. Annette Thornhill has recently published an excellent source to get you started on your own search entitled *Ask Your Doctor, Ask Yourself: How to Challenge Your Medical Care and Still Get Along with Your Doctor* (Gloucester, Massachusetts: Para Research, Inc., 1986). When I go to the library, I look in the card catalog under the particular subject heading, then I sort through stacks of books on the subject of interest, selecting the few I really want to read.

Another very practical thing I have done is call hotline telephone numbers for appropriate referrals. I placed myself on mailing lists of the support groups for people with my illness. In addition, I made important information available to my friends and my family.

In my searches for knowledge about health, illness, death, and dying with various illnesses, I have found an assortment of good news, bad news, and no news at all. Sometimes having more knowledge only added to my confusion. At other times, I was pleased to know my decisions were well studied. I came to realize that test results are considered "normal" based on a range of numbers, and I learned never to act hastily on the basis of a single test.

You can demystify the results of a variety of tests by learning what they are used for and by doing some tests yourself. A lot of pharmaceutical companies are making test kits available for over-the-counter purchase. The second opinion you get could be your own! For more information on tests you can do, read, *Do It Yourself Medical Testing: More than 160 Tests You Can Do at Home*, by Cathey Pinckney and Edward Pinckney (New York: Facts-on-File Publications, 1983). Be sure to get done the lab work your doctor recommends right at the beginning. This is important because you will need a basis of comparison for future test results. The most common ones include blood pressure, which can be used to diagnose the risk of stroke and heart disease. There are other commonly used tests. Serum cholesterol levels in high levels increases the risk of the clogging of the arteries with fatty deposits. Red blood cell count can be used to determine anemia, indicated by a low count. Low hemoglobin, a protein that carries oxygen in the blood and gives red blood cells their color, is another indication of anemia. Don't forget that what is most important about these tests is their use over a period of time. The interpretation of lab results must be in the context of a series of these tests, and some blood tests are more important to your illness than others. White blood cell counts that are higher than normal may indicate that the body is fending off

20

infection. The white blood cell differential is a test to determine what percentage of the total white blood cell count is composed of each of the white cell types; this test can help determine if an infection is bacterial or viral. The types of white cells and their ratios to one another also reveal important information about your body's ability to fend for itself. Blood glucose tests are used to diagnose hypoglycemia. Sedimentation rate can tell you if your red cells are heavier than normal, which could be the result of disease progression.

You should get familiar with these basic tests; in the new world you occupy, this is like getting weather reports. It may seem strange and uncomfortable at first, but only at first. Start learning about these tests by having your doctor explain them. Ask your doctor to refer you to other sources for details. If you still want more information, then go to a library or bookstore and get it. Don't hesitate to ask a friend to go for you; this information gathering can help them, too. Your local library can be a useful resource for further reading on technical information about diagnoses and prescriptions. Look in the card catalog under medical books or the particular diagnosis you have been given. A reference librarian can help you pinpoint the sources needed to find the information you are looking for. You may need to consult *Medical and Health Care Books and Serials in Print*, published annually by Bowker, Co., in New York, which lists all the medical publications available. Go directly to the index in the back and find the diagnosis you are interested in. You might want to take a loose-leaf notebook with you and write down everything that appears on the subject.

If you want to learn the details of a particular illness, look at the *Merck Manual*, 14th Edition (Rahway, New Jersey: Merck & Co., 1986). This book is a tremendous resource. It describes the cause of most illnesses, their pathology, and the symptoms usually displayed. This book also gives basic information about how a specific diagnosis might be made, and what prognosis you can expect for a given disease. The *Merck Manual* describes standard treatments for most illnesses. You can supplement this knowledge of your illness by reading current articles about it; use the *Cumulative Index Medicus* (Bethesda, Maryland: National Library of Medicine, 1984) for all that was written on the particular subject for the entire year.

In addition, the *Physicians' Desk Reference*, or PDR (Oradell, New Jersey: Medical Economics Co., 1987), reports details annually and with periodic updates about government-approved prescription drugs currently prescribed. It is especially useful for understanding what dosage is normally given, and what side effects are most common. If you are taking more than one medication, you should consult the *PDR* to make sure they don't counteract or collide in some way. Another excellent source for information about drugs is called *Advice for the Patient: Drug Information in Lay Language*, 7th Edition (Rockville, Maryland: U.S. Pharmacopeial Convention, Inc., 1987). This book gives you appropriate cautions, lists of side effects, and advice on how to take prescription drugs in common terms. It explains what bad effects you should watch out for and why.

You may need to ask a specialist or a medical society for information about experimental treatments and drugs from other countries. Consult a reference librarian in your hospital's medical library for references. Teaching hospitals can also provide you with information about drugs that are prescribed in other countries.

Going to the library and arming oneself with knowledge is certainly valuable. Yet, there will be times when having a partner or a buddy—like the unions did in the 1930s to help someone trying to get welfare— makes it easier. It's easier, I think, for the second person to be an advocate, and it's easier to have someone (or even a couple of friends or family members) who go with you, who ask questions, who take notes, and with whom you can discuss things afterward. You can also involve your caring partner in helping you make a list of the symptoms you have had over the past few days, which are important to discuss with the doctor. You must be prepared to communicate honestly with your doctor about your symptoms before you can expect an adequate response.

Another very practical way to know what you need to know is to ask your doctor to supply your records. You should have access to a complete set of your medical records. Make sure your doctor is willing to make your records available upon your request. It may not be necessary or desirable to demand a copy of your medical records after every lab test or every visit. I take a loose-leaf notebook with me each time I see the doctor so I can take my own notes rather than requesting his records each time. This has the twofold advantage of giving me a sense of control over what is going on and of confronting the fact that I am undergoing medical tests. But when I have to see a specialist I take my records with me. It can save a lot of time and effort if you have copies of recent lab results with you for a new or different doctor.

Having a life-threatening illness demands that you be an informed participant in your own medical care. In the words of John Stuart Mill, ". . . each is the proper guardian of his own health, whether bodily, or mental and spiritual." It is *your* life. You do not have to give up in dread, or throw your hands in the air with despair. Each of the activities and exercises I have described in this chapter is aimed at helping you make more effective medical decisions while handling the impact of a terminal diagnosis. Even when "the stream is up," it is possible to face these crises and empower yourself. You have the personal power to be effective at influencing your life and death. Be strong, but don't forget to look for the company of the people within your heart's reach. They may need you, too. You do not have to be alone, but you can be when you need.

Just as the willow bends,
you can journey ahead with dignity and
grace.

TWO

STIGMA:

Other People's Reactions to You and Your Illness

The arid autumn heat made wearing my sport jacket seem foolish so I took it off. I was somewhat prepared, having bought flesh-colored bandages to cover the biopsy incision that lay just beyond the reach of my shirt's short sleeve. I was representing Stanford University as a Foreign Student Advisor at an International Institute of Education event for foreign scholars studying at Stanford, the University of California, and other institutions in the San Francisco Bay Area.

I stood at poolside, listening to conversations in different languages. But today my usual confidence was shaken by the fear that my medical condition might be discovered. I imagined others avoiding me. Momentarily gazing into the pool's reflections, I thought of how my diagnosis of cancer would disrupt casual conversation.

I was snapped out of my reverie by the invitation to be seated for lunch. I took my assigned seat amidst a variety of foreign scholars. The woman seated to my left was a tall and lean Rhodes scholar from Germany. She quickly engaged me in a lively discussion of her experiences with sexism in various cultures, but I felt an unfamiliar awkwardness in making conversation with new people.

These recollections are among the first experiences I had of being aware of the stigma of my illness. It was during the week between biopsy and diagnosis, when the possibility became real that I might have cancer. I did have an undeniable mark that indicated skin cancer. Among my informed friends and those co-workers who knew of my condition I sensed a quickly evolving negative attitude. I felt the "shame" of having blemished skin; I felt discredited, deviant. I felt that I no longer controlled important information about myself, and feared that others could see the yet-to-come diagnosis in my eyes.

Perhaps you have had some prior experience with stigma? Can you recall any social situations where you might have been embarrassed, discredited, or stigmatized? Some people acquire nicknames that hurt, like "tubby" or "four-eyes." If you have experienced being the target of a blaming process from people forming a stereotype of you, then you already know how others can treat you once they know of your stigmatizing mark. A common ingredient to these situations is that it seems your basic integrity is at stake. It feels like who we are is in sharp contrast to who others think we are. People lean on their anticipations, demanding we behave as if we had the particular qualities they expect of persons with a terminal illness.

The discrediting effect of stigma can be very extensive. Whole groups of personality attributes and behaviors can be assigned to you as a member of a stigmatized group. Unless we act in a way that is concretely in opposition to the personality type assigned to us, other people's strategy will eventually produce the behavior in us that they expect. For example, a friend of mine often takes out her wallet and makes it clear she is about to pay for dinner as the waiter approaches; otherwise, this situation carries the assumption that I get the check.

There are emotional aspects of stigma, based on negative attitudes usually called discrimination or prejudice. Your feelings in response to negative attitudes are not only negative, but they are also out of proportion to any real threat and thus feel out of place. The "bigot mood" carries an overall negative evaluation of you that is so intense, it feels frighteningly hostile. You feel that you are a scapegoat, being treated as though you don't have inalienable rights. Sometimes people do react to frustrating situations with anger, placing blame for their problems on some defenseless "goats." Often, this displaced hostility is rationalized and justified by stereotyping. The situation of your illness is fertile ground for scapegoating. Aggression can be directed without guilt, especially if the illness can be blamed on behaviors that are judged morally reprehensible, like smoking or unsafe sex. When illness is stigmatized, particularly those illnesses that are life-threatening, prejudiced people tend to blame the victim.

You may experience avoidance by others because they see you as a danger now. Peril is that dimension of stigma that focuses on the dangers posed by stigmatized individuals. In the case of a terminal illness, the question often includes issues of contagion. History tells the powerful story of the "Black Death" plague that raged throughout Europe, illustrating the extreme medical danger that some infectious conditions can generate, with their accompanying reactions of social rejection and hostility.

Leprosy still strikes terror in most people, prompting fears of contagion. The leper colony in Kalaupapa, Hawaii, contained over 1,000 quarantined men, women, and children by 1900, and was reported to have 125 people living there still in 1981. Other conditions that elicit the fear of contamination or contagion include those that are occasionally contagious, like tuberculosis. In addition, conditions like cancer that pose no actual threat of transmission from the afflicted to the observer may generate fears of contagion.

I have frequently noticed the absence of a handshake from individuals who are unrealistically fearful of physical contamination. Adding insult to injury, these people also give in to their fears of social rejection because of mere association with me. Individuals who would be "clean" and normally acceptable to others might acquire, by association with me, some of the socially degrading characteristics of my illness. This leads to their avoidance of the stigmatized person. The avoidance is particularly obvious when so-called normal people won't touch an ill person. This fear of association and contamination makes it especially important for the ill person to be touched by loved ones.

In our society it is not only the stigmatized person who is socially outcast, but also those who are associated or acquainted with the stigmatized person. My friends have told me that even a casual walk down the street with me can stigmatize them. Social degradation is transmitted in this way, causing a significant handicap for the newly diagnosed person who would like to return to the community and live among old friends. This kind of fear can exist independent of any real possibility of contagion. I don't usually correct these kinds of fears, unless the person is very important to me.

Don't be surprised if others aren't eager to have casual discussions about the meaning of death. The subject of death and dying has made only modest social advances as an acceptable topic of conversation. When you try to talk about death with a friend, you may suddenly find them talking about chicken salad! It isn't farfetched to imagine a guest suddenly overwhelmed by the fact that you are living with a deadly disease, and that guest becoming physically ill to the point of fainting and/or vomiting upon first being confronted with the fact of your impending death.

There was a time in our history when people held

a constant fascination with death. In *Death and the Middle Ages*, T. S. Boase (New York: McGraw-Hill, 1972) wrote of this period, when the Christians had an "art of dying," and there was a "dance of death." During the plague years, the common belief was that the plague was due to an international conspiracy of Jewry to poison Christendom. The Jews, under torture, confessed to poisoning German wells and incriminated others. Thousands of Jews were butchered and burnt. Often the weak and unpopular are cast as degenerates who provoked divine punishment in the guise of an appropriate disease. The persecution of minorities, particularly Jews, but also lepers, grave diggers, and foreigners, was common in Europe during the plague.

The influenza pandemic of 1918 was known throughout the world. Commercial advertisers took advantage of the epidemic in several ways. One Danish newspaper carried no less than 117 advertisements for different kinds of mouthwash. Medical practice and advice varied greatly in 1918. The New Zealand Health Department advised people to "go to bed between warm blankets," while other New Zealand doctors said to "go to bed between wet sheets." Emergency inhalation chambers were used in Venice, California, Spain, and New Zealand; these were windowless huts into which people were forced and made to inhale sulfur for twelve seconds. The result: Those who passed through the chambers were more likely to come down with the flu.

Strange beliefs and practices did not belong only to

the medicine man. The common man, in whatever nation, had a wealth of superstition. The citizens of Meng Feng in China tried to divert the flu spirit with firecrackers and red paper mottoes in a fake New Year's Day celebration. In Tibet, the belief most common was that if a sick man slept too much, more devils would enter his body. Thus, the lamas pounded drums and clashed symbols in the streets day and night! New Zealanders would accept only brown medicine, in harmony with their own skin color. In Poland, two young orphans were united in a "sacrificial wedding" in the Jewish cemetery. The rabbi stood beside the grave of the latest flu victim as the orphans pledged their vows in an attempt to exorcise the plague. One man in Yingshang, China, pledged that if God would spare the man's sick mother from death, he would sacrifice his only son. After the man's mother was cured, the man publicly threw his one-year-old son into a hot cauldron of incense.

Stereotyping people who are ill as if they deserved their illness is often done by those who need to justify their own negative feelings about the illness. And, unfortunately, this stereotyping does not always diminish among people who interact frequently with ill persons. In some cases, frequent exposure to people with a particular illness will result in a realization that traits and behaviors previously thought to be common among people with this illness are overgeneralized and untrue. On the other hand, some stereotyped beliefs among the helping professionals are harder to change, leaving patients feeling that they must have done something to deserve a terminal illness. These stereotypes are based partly on accurate information and partly on the medical personnel's need to explain their own otherwise unjustifiable feelings and reactions. In addition, social workers and health care workers often have a general stance toward terminally ill patients that smacks of "poor you." I have often walked away from interactions with health care workers with the distinct feeling that I have been patronized.

What caused you to get sick? Where did your illness spring from? These are questions that reveal another critical aspect of stigma that will determine your experience with your illness. Social beliefs about your particular illness will most likely be widespread. The relationship between social and scientific advances is very close when it comes to health. Clearly, the advances in social attitudes toward cancer that have been made parallel medical discovery. We are fairly certain that cancer is not catching. Today, AIDS is the Pandora's box bursting forth with ugly stereotypes about contagion and risk.

Illness can force a more extensive sharing of personal information than you want. Aspects of your life that have been hidden in the past or relatively unimportant can be suddenly exposed. You may find it helpful to distinguish between responsibility for causing your illness, and responsibility for maintaining it. Similarly, one can distinguish between taking responsibility for past behavior, like smoking, that causes lung cancer, and current behavior, like not smoking, which may positively influence the outcome of one's illness.

Your role in causing your illness has an important influence in the stigmatizing process. Some people will treat you better when you are judged not to be responsible for your condition. On the other hand, when you are believed to be responsible for causing your illness, some form of punishment is likely to be involved in the way others respond to you. One reason for this is the common belief that, since it is a just world, the sufferers must deserve their fate. Some people will see you as having brought your misfortune upon yourself through laziness or sin. This belief may wipe away both their guilt and the disagreeable prospect of having to give time, care, or money.

Sometimes stigmatized people will behave according to the expectations of their social stigma. A person can internalize another's belief about him or her. The person may even look for examples in his own behavior and character that would confirm the social stereotype or stigma. This internalization sometimes has the profound effect of creating self-hate, self-denial, and an overall fear of trusting one's emotions. In addition, when the stigmatized person is feeling down and out, he may look inwardly for evidence to support a negative image of himself. I call this "beating yourself up." The result can be the development of a complete identity that has been externally defined. You may even believe that you don't deserve to be treated with courtesy and fairness. Take care that you do not grow to believe you are what others say about people with your illness. The consequences of giving in to the negative beliefs and expectations of others can be stopped by asserting your individuality. Don't get stuck in some endless inward search for the reason others may mistreat or misperceive you. The reasons are more likely to be found in *their* character than in yours. You know yourself better than anyone else does, so hold fast!

But you will have to consider your role realistically in becoming ill. Face it—if your illness is one you contracted after birth, you may be somewhat responsible for it. You may find that it is difficult not to dwell on self-blaming thoughts. Maybe you smoked too many cigarettes, ate too much butter, or had unsafe sex.

A useful way to cope with memories that create guilt in you is to acknowledge that *at one time* in the past, you did engage in activities that you may or may not have known would damage your health. Don't use that as a reason to continue doing health-damaging things, however. Your acknowledgment of which activities and behaviors are going to make you live longer and which ones will not is enough for now.

Use this as a time to define the activities and relationships that promote your will to stay among the living. Blaming yourself or others for your illness may increase your suffering. Warning: Putting responsibility for your health in the hands of others can deny you the opportunity to handle this event to the best of your ability. It can make you helpless to influence the outcome of your situation, which is living with dying.

Now, you can move on to dwell on a new thought: "What can I do to be responsible for how my illness shapes the remainder of my life?" None of us can erase the past, but we can all take responsibility for how much we let the illness determine the quality and values in our remaining days and nights.

When you are dwelling on a negative thought that would threaten your sense of self-worth, deliberately replace that thought with one that emphasizes responsible actions today. For example, if you are thinking, "I deserve to die for all the things I've done," then *stop that thought!* Replace it with, "I may have behaved in ways that damaged my health in my past, but I now have some time to do things differently." Go on then to acknowledge that all of us deserve to live for our opportunities and happiness. Your goal here is to accept who you are and where you've been, while holding on to possibilities for happiness.

There are several other tips on taking responsibility for your health while diminishing blame. This will help to reduce negative self-blame: Recall some of the good things you have done that a person who *deserves* to die just couldn't have done. You are apt to discover that you have done things in your life that you can be proud of. Also, you can make a list of your accomplishments and give it a heading. For example, if you are especially proud of your career achievements, your list might be entitled, "Early Career Achievement

Award." Accomplishments may be job related or not; In fact, many of the accomplishments you should consider listing will be personal successes and emotional breakthroughs. After you have made your list of accomplishments, look for things you have done that contradict the notion that "You deserve to die."

The daily hassles and crises of a life-threatening illness can cause a lot of stress. This stress often results in a sense of confusion, a breakdown in communication. There is an inherent danger of emotional overreaction for all persons involved.

Having a terminal illness heightens the frequency of doubt and conflict in one's life. You may have mixed feelings about your illness, or the way you acquired your illness. You may have mixed feelings about your financial and social situation. You may sense in others an ambivalence in their feelings about death. In many cases, social stigma results in hostility, prejudice, and discrimination. In the case of a life-threatening illness, the stigma more often results in avoidance.

On the other hand, you may doubt the genuineness of care-giving from friends and family. You may feel good that they are nearby, and feel badly that they are taking time and energy from their own lives. You may feel in conflict because you experience both positive and negative emotions toward others. These effects of stigma give way to doubt: Do people pity you, or just feel morally obligated to care for you? If you believe that others naturally resent the burden you impose, you may grow to suspect former friends of maintaining the friendship out of pity. This situation is fraught with the danger of overreaction. Take the time needed to check out these perceptions with the people in question before you take the initiative in severing long-standing friendships.

You should be aware that the kind of danger or threat experienced by a "normal" person interacting with a stigmatized person can take many forms. The emaciated and dying cancer patient may make us starkly aware that a similar fate can befall us. Danger, in its many forms, is the most fundamental characteristic of stigmatizing interactions. In addition, people who are sick are in low power positions within society, and are often viewed as irresponsible. The social role of the sick and dying may be founded in the perception by both the healthy and ill that the limitations imposed by the illness are much more incapacitating than they are in reality.

There are some common social rules that deal with ill people as a category. The social roles are less responsible for people who are expected to die soon from a life-threatening illness. I have observed a variety of sick roles and scripts for interacting with others. Each one has different implications. For example, if the script of the sick person is a situation that provides the threat of contracting your illness, you may feel intense anxiety and see physical avoidance from others. I believe this may contribute to our desire to avoid contact with victims of cancer and those with skin disorders.

When the sickness is seen as terminal, yet another script is involved. The desire to avoid the terminally ill may follow from vague fears associated with the recognition of our own mortality. On the other hand, I have seen people acting from a realistic desire not to get involved in a relationship destined for separation and grief.

Stigma builds about us as we live with a life-threatening illness, until all our relationships are shaped by it in one way or another. Long-term relationships are especially influenced by the ongoing strains of stigma. I have watched many couples deal with the stigma of terminal illness. Coping is made easier by open and honest conversations about how each person views the illness. Relationships are embedded within a social system, and each person must make their adjustment to the particular illness accordingly. Even the most isolated relationship is not immune to media messages that tell us how society in general perceives an illness.

Specifically, those illnesses associated with moral weakness affect the couple's adjustment and commitment to one another. AIDS is certainly an example, being stereotypically associated with intimate contact other than monogamy. So, the personal problems faced by members of relationships in which one of the parties has been diagnosed with a terminal illness include their possibly different and sometimes conflicting reactions to it. The illness will have a special meaning for each person.

The very basis of our emotional and social relationships becomes open for redefinition. New roles may be forced upon the couple, such as who brings home the bacon and who fries it up. Sometimes the individuals involved will break apart and terminate their relationship. This may be done out of a fear of losing a loved one coupled with a preference for breaking up rather than facing death.

Couples with honest and open communication are usually thought to be those who are most successful in dealing with intense strain. In my own experiences, I have seen that openness about conflicting feelings may be helpful, and perhaps necessary.

One of the first lessons I learned about the ways others may treat me when they learn of my illness is that any blemish can be made more or less obvious. Some symptoms and side effects of treatment can be more easily concealed than others. Some characteristics of the illness may create a physical mark that makes it obvious to all, while others remain completely undetected. You will discover that the visibility of your illness can play a central role in producing a negative social reception. How much you have to deal with stigmatizing reactions to you will depend a lot on how obvious your illness is.

Since my diagnosis, I have become acquainted with how people who consider my illness a form of ugliness treat me. People seem to believe that what is beautiful is good and what is ugly is bad. Ugly or disfigured or frightening-looking people are expected to do evil things! It helped me to learn that in general unattractive people are treated differently and more negatively than those who are attractive. Ugly or physically marked people are clearly disadvantaged. If you are seen by others as ugly, you will feel their negative emotions immediately; and you may also have to cope with the pains of isolation over a long term. The damage caused by others avoiding you include that you feel cruelly rejected over and over.

I have noticed powerful conditions that cause social rejection for me as a terminally ill person. My terminal condition is progressively crippling and deforming, and is not curable. The fact that my condition will deteriorate until I finally die causes a lot of rejection. The degree of stigma others assign to my illness gets more negative as the illness advances. Society beliefs, your beliefs, and the facts of your illness each play their own role in causing social rejection.

One of the many ways in which social rejection rears its ugly head can be seen when forming new relationships. Many people won't become friends with a dying person. I have learned to encourage a detached compassion in some people, playing down their possible responsibilities to me. When I need a health service, I am explicit in seeking appropriate care It seems to relieve others when they know that I will take responsibility for my illness episodes and my dying experience.

You may sense a disruptiveness that hinders, strains, and adds to the difficulty of your relationships. The more visible, dangerous, and aesthetically displeasing the symptoms and side effects of your illness, the more difficult it will become to have smooth personal interactions. You may find your interactions with others uncertain and unpredictable. This happens in part because the illness calls attention to itself and away from other characteristics you have. Danger! Your illness can replace you. That's right, and some ill people talk openly about having to assert that *they are not their illness*.

Illnesses become disruptive when they block or distort the communications process. A common way for illness to block communications is by the sheer physical sight of illness. When so-called normal people believe they are being unobserved, they stare more at a strikingly different or unusual than a more usual person. Visibly stigmatized people attract the lust of the eye. In general, people both want to stare at unusual people or events, and yet adhere to the social norm of not staring. This is particularly true when the one being stared at may be hypersensitive to stares. In this way, disruptiveness is caused and communication blocked.

Each of us has some aesthetic sense of what is beautiful or pleasing. Amputee children get rejected by other children for aesthetic reasons. Similarly, dwarfs are rejected socially. Aesthetics stirs a primitive emotional response sometimes called a gut reaction. For example, the gut reaction we have when we meet someone whose face has been horribly marked with cancer and weight loss is immediate. Our impulse to retreat from the negative aesthetic impact is nearly unavoidable.

Be patient with your friends and loved ones as they come to terms with their own reactions. You may help by reminding them of how difficult it has been for you to acknowledge how normal such a gut reaction is. The first time you look in the mirror at yourself after severe weight loss, when you realize that you can't turn any more pale, you feel sick—even dizzy. With close friends be persistent—you can resolve the doubts and confusions surrounding your illness and others' reactions to it. Talking openly with those you care for is absolutely necessary to establish a comfortable rapport that will enable you to cope with your situation.

The decision of whom to tell and how to tell about your illness is not a singular act, done once and for all. You will be making that decision over and over, and you can become quite effective at it. Your social life might even be reasonably satisfactory, despite your potentially disruptive problem. I discovered that nurturing positive reactions from others depended on whether and how I disclosed my cancer diagnosis and the ongoing nature of living with AIDS. I have also found that the particular circumstances of any interaction—say a doctor's visit verses a lunch date in a restaurant with a professional acquaintance—require different degrees of openness. Total openness is not always possible or necessary.

Be careful about how much personal information

you share with others. One way to do this is to stay aware of how much sharing of personal information they engage in. Mutual disclosure is a better thing than one-sided disclosure. In fact, if you tell someone who hardly knows you too much too fast, you may be viewed with suspicion. You may even drive them away in a panic.

Remind yourself that you deserve to be treated with common courtesy and respect. If you have a good reason to be angry, then say so! Cruel responses to you gain impetus from a "just deserts" argument. This argument isn't about a one-course meal, mind you. It can be used as evidence that you are being justly repaid for some mistake, indiscretion, or evil act. When this happens to you, assert yourself as effectively as you can in that situation. For example, if someone says, "I told you not to smoke, your disease is no surprise," you can tell them that you understand that, and then say whatever else their comment makes you want to say to them. If you need to learn new ways to assert yourself, start by describing the situations you imagine you might be in, then rehearse new ways you want to deal with them.

If your illness is concealable, you will have some opportunities that those afflicted with an obvious problem do not have. First of all, you can choose the proper time to disclose your situation. You have an opportunity to demonstrate your worth and humanity before the illness makes that process more difficult or impossible. In general, both physically ill and socially

43

stigmatized individuals who can conceal that mark identifying their affliction will do just that. There are immediate and powerful rewards for "passing as normal." A proper place in social conversation is given to the handsome and fit. Yet, I would not say that if a mark of illness or the side effects of treatment can be successfully concealed, go ahead and conceal it without concern about the effect it will have on any of your friendships. There may be obvious and awkward effects of hiding it, such as wearing a hat or a wig. Also, it may engender guilt and shame in you, even if the other person does not know the truth of your condition.

Concealing your illness from long-term and close relationships plays a different role than it does in initial encounters and short-term relationships. Here is another advantage to concealing your illness until you want to disclose it: Your family and friends can talk with people who are important to them, telling others of your condition as needed. This can help your spouse, family members, and friends to manage any awkwardness or embarrassment they may confront as they talk with others. It is *not* possible to conceal your illness and its ramifications from those who are in close and repeated contact. It could even be argued that it is not fair to do so. Family members and old friends will almost invariably become aware of your condition.

You may find that the more evident and nonconcealable your illness becomes, the more it seems to interfere with such life functions as moving about, working, and caring for yourself. On the other hand, if the illness cannot be seen, you may maintain normal functioning. In the long run, hiding your illness from mere acquaintances will make your life easier, because others are not adversely affected by your appearance. Also, they will not be burdened with concerns about your needs, or make special efforts because of your condition. Try to remain flexible with what you allow yourself to need from special friends and loved ones. Your honest flexibility will promote a healthier adaptation for all those concerned by your health crisis.

Hiding your illness and the events surrounding it will not be a carefree enterprise. One problem raised by concealing your diagnosis and illness is that of trust. If you are someone who seems outwardly quite normal but is later found to have AIDS, you will not only appear blighted by a heinous condition, but may also appear deceitful and dangerous.

If your illness is visible it may sometimes be more manageable and permit easier adaptation for all concerned than if it is unseen. In general, stigmatized individuals who believe others are aware of their blemish are less adversely affected, because they are less tense and less self-conscious than those who are unsure about whether their condition is known or not.

Take care of your self-worth, lest guilt and shame become debilitating. These negative feelings about your own illness can inhibit your usual social behavior. For example, you may find yourself fearing discovery. If a long-term relationship with another individual is contemplated, you should face this issue head-on. A word to the wise: Your fear of discovery can breed an anticipation of catastrophic social consequences that is worse than what might result from open and honest disclosure, and that fear will have its own impact. Clearly, your social interactions will be affected even when others are entirely ignorant of your condition.

There may be situations in which your illness is known by someone without your realizing it. When this happens, you can become the victim of the stigmatizing process. When another's hidden expectations of us somehow makes us act as if we are the person they treat us like, the old "self-fulfilling prophesy" is at work. I have frequently been asked by people, when in this situation, a set of questions that have to do with common notions about people with the illness I have. When I am asked about my personal life in this manner, I state openly that I am offended. For instance, if a person asks me if I still have sexual relations with a lot of other people, or if I still do drugs, I let him or her know that I have been in a faithful relationship for several years, and extend an invitation to look at my forearms for needle tracks. This direct confrontation of assumptions usually heightens the other person's awareness.

Other situations make me feel like I'm being dealt a stacked deck of cards. You may not always know when another is aware of your condition. Even though you may not know for sure whether another person knows about your diagnosis, you might detect unexpected patterns in the other's behavior, such as keeping his physical distance or making off-color remarks. Such as the day I went to work out at the Stanford University weight room. I was pumping iron just as I had as an undergraduate, in the old days. I was feeling great that day. It had been two years since my diagnosis with AIDS, and I had not been to the gym since then. Then an old colleague walked up and deliberately exclaimed, "Lon, you look great! I thought you had AIDS?" That corner of the weight room cleared out fast! Gossip had reached the ears of the old co-worker, only to be hurled viciously into public realm, intended to keep me constrained within the stigma of my illness.

There are some very practical things to do when you are sure that others are aware of your illness. You can attempt to disavow or minimize the illness, its symptoms and treatment side effects. When someone asks how you are feeling, you don't have to tell all the details. Take some control of what you do talk about with others, asking about *their* life, too. Explain that you don't feel downtrodden and handicapped, but you can understand how others may assume you do.

There are a lot of coping skills and tactics to use daily as you confront stigma. Protecting the integrity of your character from social assassination will require you to challenge attitudes that blame and punish you for your illness. I even scheduled fifteen-minute periods during which all negative thoughts were banished. I would simply focus all my thoughts and my feelings in a positive light. One time my schedule for positive thinking was interrupted by a friend's visit, and I asked her to join me. This person was a classic complainer: No one suffered more than she! But, during the fifteen minutes we spent thinking, speaking, and acting positively, she, too, benefited. It brought us into a meeting of meanings about what was positive and possible. Spending time looking at the best of life, the good parts, gave her ideas she needed to improve her love relationships and family ties.

You may want to learn ways to assert yourself when confronted by stigma. You can practice ways to cope with different situations. For example, imagine how a situation might be structured to make you powerless, then color in your description of the situation with your feelings about how you fear others may treat you. Authors Sharon Bower and Gordon Bower have written a practical guide to becoming more assertive entitled *Asserting Yourself* (Menlo Park, California: Addison-Wesley, 1976), which has a unique approach to gaining self-esteem and confidence in expressing yourself effectively and forthrightly. It is based on the humanist view that each person must take the responsibility for creating the quality of his or her relationships with others. The Bowers suggest a program that uses the notion of a "script." When you feel troubled about some problem, write a script to solve it assertively. There are four basic rules for assertive scripts, including:

1. Describe the other person's behavior objectively, using concrete terms; describe the specific time, place, and frequency of the other's actions, but don't guess at his or her motives.

2. Express your feelings calmly and in a positive manner; direct yourself to the particular actions rather than attacking the entire character of the person.

3. Specify what change you desire in the person's behavior, making small requests that do not ask for too large or too many changes. Be clear about the action you want to see stopped, and the ones you want to have instead. State specific behaviors that you would be willing to change, if appropriate.

4. Let the person know you are not ashamed to talk about rewards and penalties by making the consequences explicit. Reward positive change in a way that is meaningful to the other person. Select a punishment that is appropriate to the person and the behavior that you would be willing to carry out.

There are many ways to confront stigma, but none relieves the tension that thickens the air of such situations like stark humor. One mother of a handicapped daughter told me that she refused to hide her child in shame. Even though the preteen child was unaware of the stares of others, her mother noticed each one with simmering anger. One day, tired of the rude stares from others, the mother confronted an onlooker with, "What's wrong, did she leave home with her head on backward again?" This woman did not consider herself assertive before, but she learned how to be.

You must learn ways to stand up for yourself. You probably know by now that others may act differently toward you as an ill person. Diagnosis makes us aware that we now possess an illness that some others regard with stigmatizing disdain. It is nonetheless hard to tell who will be more likely than another to degrade us. Most of us find this type of situation highly anxiety-provoking. Don't let these situations lead you to look constantly for evidence that you are being put down. Insist that others treat you with respect, but don't react by suddenly blurting out your rage. Take time to confirm your perceptions and act accordingly. Set aside some time to write out a script for how you would like to handle the situation, talk it over with a friend, and then try it out.

When others treat me as a failure, they are often confusing their perceptions, so that physical sickness represents personality weakness. Some people will shun the visibly ill as though they were bad. And many people have a problem making any kind of binding agreement with a terminally ill person. Still, you can become so comfortable with your own circumstances that you no longer lose your cool and react to others who are ill equipped to cope with you, but pause and act according to your adult behavior.

You might find it helpful to talk with another person who has the same illness, to sharpen your awareness of these stigmatizing situations. You can learn to perceive prejudice in a way that gives you control of the situation. Identify the things that trigger others' stereotypical beliefs about you and your illness. It is true that a raging bigot is easier to spot, and easier to deal with, than a person with a liberal facade. Yet, a few of the right questions can get the answers you want about the prejudice they may have toward you and your illness. For instance, asking others what they know about the illness is a start. Or you can inquire about specific issues, such as how they believe you might have become ill.

Another practical thing to do when you feel you are being stigmatized is to assert yourself in ways that are in contrast to what is expected. Be helpful to others, rather than helpless in general. Be self-reliant when the chips are down. You can demonstrate that you can still help meet some of the needs you have without becoming totally dependent on others. By acting on your own behalf, you can persuade others that the unfavorable characteristics generally associated with the illness you have are not true in your case.

You might want to make your life easier by avoiding so-called normals. You can chose to socialize only with people who have the same illness you have. There are times when this is valuable; it's a relief to have our own space. That is not the only solution, though, and it has drawbacks. For example, you will grow to feel even more isolated from society in general. Some of the other ill people will not be as sick as you are, giving rise to negative reactions in you. Similarly, comparing yourself to persons who are sicker than you can create a sense of dread in yourself.

There are times when the most practical thing to do is the least comfortable for you. For example, letting others stare at you might help them, but it doesn't feel very good to us. I have noticed when in a wheelchair that after giving others the opportunity to look unobtrusively at me, I was subsequently avoided less. By permitting someone to look on comfortably, they could almost become familiar and accepting of what they saw. You may be able to put others at ease by allowing them to stare. For example, if you pretend to be sleeping or simply look away so as not to notice their stares, the other person can look long enough to reduce the disruptive conflict. The consequence of giving them permission to stare is that they're more comfortable.

Take charge of selecting your network of friends carefully. Start by exerting influence over the time selected to reveal your illness to the people close to you. Many of your friends will be well aware of the social consequences of interacting with you. Some will continue the relationship through loyalty. Others are likely to seek an avenue of escape from the uncomfortable dilemma. You may sense them drifting away from you. They may leave your company abruptly, overwhelmed and unable to cope. Some of your social contacts will gradually disengage themselves from your life. This kind of experience can make you ever so conscious of the burden you impose on others by socializing with them. Make your choices about with whom you will be involved based on your feelings about their ability and willingness to see you clearly and accept who you are. A desire not to hurt your friends may lead you to terminate old relationships, but they may understand your situation more than you think. In fact, they may know you more than you give them credit for.

The stigma of your illness will be overcome by some people by their true image of you. Consider the following words from Margery Williams' book, *The Velveteen Rabbit* (New York: Avon Books, 1975):

> "It doesn't happen all at once," said the Skin Horse. "You become. It takes a long time. That's why it doesn't often happen to people who break easily, or have sharp edges, or who have to be carefully kept. Generally, by the time you are Real, most of your hair has been loved off, and your eyes drop out and you get loose in the joints and very shabby. But these things don't matter at all, because once you are Real you can't be ugly, except to people who don't understand."

Many people will understand the situation you are in and not see you as ugly, so let's not forget that it is possible to achieve open acknowledgment of your terminal illness and its accompanying stigma. You can place your illness in a constructive context. One way to do this is by presenting yourself in a way that prevents your illness from gaining some sort of master status in your personality. Put your best foot forward. Take credit for your accomplishments, for who you are and for what you do best.

You will gain confidence as you master more situations by maintaining control over them. If you feel a loved one has a confused view of you and your illness, ask them to work it through with you. Ask them to talk about why your illness makes them uncomfortable, while explaining to them how your illness can be used to put you down. Explain how certain social situations make you feel "like your nose is out of joint." You can effectively turn the stigma of your illness inside out.

Be gutsy and don't let go of who you are!

THREE

COPING:

How You Handle Daily Living Affects Your Health and Morale

I'm glad to have some time alone, I thought to myself. I had been lying awake in the silence of the night for what seemed to be hours. It was five o'clock in the morning when the summer sun finally reflected from the tip of the pyramid-shaped TransAmerica building that makes San Francisco's skyline unmistakable. I had a flawless view of downtown from my hospital bed, stirring in me the conflicting feelings of being simultaneously isolated from and connected to the "real" world.

The night nurse tiptoed into my isolation room right on schedule, finishing her last round before the day crew began. She plugged me in to another bottle of seemingly harmless clear liquid. "Please slow down the dripping," I asked, "it burns a lot." She reduced the flow of the insidious but healing antibiotic, staying a few minutes to gently stroke my purple, pincushioned arms.

When she left, my mind wandered to what it would be like to survive this bout with a life-threatening infection. I suddenly felt overwhelmed by a fear of living, terrified of living with some ugly disfigurement or handicap.

I found myself grappling with questions like, "Could it be possible that some people with AIDS would live longer than others, leaving behind a battered platoon of veterans beset with horrifying memories, images of the disfigured bodies of buddies?" This isn't Korea, World War II, or Vietnam. Yet, it seemed that everywhere I looked people were stepping on land mines. How can I express my feelings? I wondered. How dare I speak of this fear of living?

I looked to my lover asleep in the cot next to my hospital bed. Billy had had such a difficult time getting to sleep last night. I did not want to wake him—not even for the spectacular views of the colorful morning sky. I thought it odd of me never to have appreciated the special moment of sunrise so much before. My desire to share the beauty of life brought tears to my eyes and chills rushed up my spine.

Last night, Billy had asked to watch me fall asleep. Now, as I rested alone, I remembered a story he had told me of his childhood. It had been tough for him to fall asleep after being forced to recite the "Now I lay me down to sleep, I pray the Lord my soul to keep, and if I die before I wake . . ." prayer every night. I sensed that he was growing to fear my sleep, which makes his nights so much longer, lying awake, thinking constantly that death may come to me as I sleep. I wished he would talk to me about his fears of my death. I wondered if he was afraid of a life without me.

I was looking at his peaceful face when he awoke, and our eyes met in one of those movie-making "We're still together and I love you more than ever" looks.

Our breakfast trays were soon delivered, which were not altogether bad, because the coffee and toast were decent. Yet, the toast was hard for me to swallow, getting stuck at the emotional lump in my throat.

"The man in the next room died last night," I said. The custodial staff was busy cleaning up his room as we spoke. We became silent, our faces saddening, as noises of furniture moving on linoleum floors overrode our thoughts.

I knew I could entrust my feelings to him. I knew we could talk honestly. I knew he was not lagging behind me in accepting the truth of my illness. Yet, I couldn't bring myself to say what we both needed to say: What we were feeling was excruciating.

It was nearly noon before I got the nerve to say that I was afraid of living with this illness. True to his character, Billy reciprocated with equal intimacy. Almost angrily, but with a face full of tears, he blurted out, "But, I'm so afraid of losing you." The sterile hospital air was colored with hues of irony.

Since that illness episode nearly three years ago, I have learned that talking about such intimate subjects as your fear of living and fear of dying with the people near and dear to you is an ongoing process. It takes time, it never ends, and it can't be finally packaged. Talking about the fear of dying inescapably leads us to talk about the fears we have about living. I recently experienced the incorrigible nature of these fears when a young man hardly in his twenties came to me after receiving his positive AIDS antibody test. I found we were tripping over his fears of living, while we struggled to define the meaning his diagnosis would have for every aspect of his life. After we talked, he understood that coping with daily living would involve his responding to the demands of his situation and to his own feelings about that situation. The event of his medical test results required him to get out of immediate danger, to see to the security of his health, job, and housing. He also started to deal with feelings of loss, depression, inadequacy, and guilt. I understood that he was in an acute phase of shock, requiring that most of his energy be directed at minimizing the stressful impact of his lab tests. He would reorganize his life and self-image gradually.

You should know that the silence of hiding your feelings from everyone can have negative consequences. Hiding feelings of fear, loss, sadness, and anger certainly can have a negative influence on your morale. You may become detached and try to forget the whole thing, going on as if nothing has happened. Hiding feelings can shape your ability to function socially, making you less effective at maintaining social relationships. Hiding your feelings can even have a negative impact on your physical health, leading you to go along with fate, believing nothing can be done. Both men and women have been studied for their reactions to hiding particular emotions, and while we each have our individual differences, neither men nor women gain health benefits from shoving their feelings under the rug.

On the other hand, don't forget to consider the consequences of your expressions, particularly the impact your anger can have on others. You may not want to express your feelings to everyone. Coping by expressing what you are feeling is a good way to seek social support, but it may be more appropriate to discuss your feelings with medical personnel and close friends than with collegues or acquaintances. The important point here is that you talk to someone who can do something concrete about the problem or tell you more about the situation. You may feel most comfortable asking a respected relative or friend for advice.

Anger and depression are probably the most common emotions we experience in response to life-threatening illness. Anger may last a few hours sometimes and a few days the next. So it is also with depression: We are more depressed at certain times than others. Anger can be used to make us aware of the real frustrations in our objective situation. It is commonly thought that young and middle-age persons facing death tend to remain angry longer than older people. There is something distinct about "facing an early grave." In most of the death and dying literature people in their mid-career are described as being more resentful than people who feel satisfied with their life, and parents are often furious at being taken from their children. Depression can result from a child's birthday, holidays, and especially a poor hospital situation. Talking about what you feel won't always be enough. You may need to permit yourself to become temporarily absorbed in that feeling. A word to the wise: Sometimes the only path that reaches the other side is through the middle. Depression can be used to gain insight about your situation and light the path to correcting the things that depress your spirit.

There are ways of coping with your feelings that may contribute to prolonging your life. Appropriate emotional expression can encourage your sense of self-control over the course of your illness. You can gain control over many of your symptoms by talking about how they make you feel. It is clear from research and anecdotal reports that people with cancer who shout and scream, when that's what a situation calls for, live longer than those who shut up and hold their pains and fears and angers inside. By talking about your fears and frustrations with your friends and care providers, you can create collaborators in your wellness. You may need to use a confrontive style of coping, expressing anger to the person who caused the problem. But you can actively participate in your social world, integrating the treatments you select with your daily living.

The beliefs you have about what kinds of feelings are okay to experience and to express are important to your health. Men and women are traditionally taught different styles of emotional response. Men are stereo-typically less expressive and more instrumental than women. Don't let these social rules and roles get in the way of your own expressiveness.

In addition, whether you are a man or a woman, you may have the general belief that feelings like anger, depression, and anxiety are bad. The source of these beliefs may be the common notion that these emotions are signs of a weak character. I have found it helpful to suspend belief about the goodness or badness (judgments) of any particular emotion. For example, when I feel hurt by another's treatment toward me, I may think it bad to be mad. But looked at from a neutral perspective, I can claim my anger as appropriate and manage to express both the hurt and the anger in ways about which I feel good. By permitting myself to ex-perience my feelings, I have been able to work through them.

I have gained emotional self-acceptance and clarity in the sense that I know what I am feeling most of the time. Perhaps most importantly, I know that my emo-tional states are bound to situations and events. This knowledge makes it possible for me to get a grip on my situation, rather than participate in my own vic-timization. It is critical for you to acknowledge that it is the facts of your illness situation, not something about your personality, that has you in quite a state.

Let's not fool ourselves about the feelings we have about our terminal diagnosis. A lot of what we feel will be unpleasant. None of us wants to accept joyfully such feelings as pain, grief, and anxiety. Our goal for handling these unpleasant emotional states must be realistic. I try to maintain the attitude that I don't want to endorse these feelings as a lifestyle; I only want to accept and integrate them as temporary side effects of the events in my immediate situation.

Expressing your feelings about what is happening to your health and to your living situation can help you grow. You can become more of who you want to be by talking about what you feel. Some of what you feel you will want to stop feeling. By purging that which falls short of what you can and want to be, you can get on with becoming all you can be. You may grow as a person in a good way, changing some things about yourself. You may even rediscover what is important in life.

At times you may feel inspired, even courageous. But it may be easier for others to hear you expressing your mental and emotional despair than to listen to your confidence or loyalty with regard to the tasks facing you. You will have to gauge how much of this tenacity-in-the-face-of-adversity others can handle. One way to do this is to ask the person if they feel you are denying the inevitable by facing the functional. After all, you *are* still alive.

It is critical that you have a safe place to express your feelings. A nonjudgmental atmosphere can help you to communicate your truths and share a common experience. This can be enriching for both of you and it can build trust. A good place may be with your spouse or a close friend. You may feel more comfortable with a mental health professional, and that is okay. You can find appropriate referrals through telephone hot lines, or by asking your primary care physician. If you are in the hospital, you can ask a nurse if they have a social worker on staff.

Another way to safely express yourself is to join a support group for persons with your illness. This can be very helpful, because you gain a sense of what a normal reaction is for people facing the illness you have. You can compare yourself with people who are in your situation, rather than compare yourself with the people you knew before you became ill. Expressing your feelings will help you to cope by temporarily getting them outside you. You can gain some objectivity by externalizing your feelings. You've got to express yourself!

You may be surprised, but you might get something positive out of your illness. One of the best ways to tap your adaptive ability is to redefine a situation or event as a challenge. You can then draw upon many emotional resources and varied coping strategies. Challenge can stimulate you to reach new and creative heights in your personal growth. But whenever you define a situation as a loss, you are likely to become depressed and despondent. And if you define a situation as a threat, you are likely to become defensive and avoiding.

Redefining the situation as a challenge can be used as a way of coping by taking direct action, and by regulating your emotions. Many ill people who view daily events as a challenge use a set of coping skills that include rational action, perseverance, positive thinking, restraint, self-adaptation, drawing strength from adversity, and humor. Irony is a good kind of humor. It reveals the striking difference between our expectations and what actually happens or exists. I have had a few belly laughs with friends over the fact that I have outlived many arguments about how long I would live. A frail and aging doctor recently pulled me aside after I had delivered a speech to his group and shared a similar experience. He had been receiving pension checks for over ten years with the words, "DO NOT CASH IF DECEASED" printed on them. He told me that he "gleefully takes his checks to the bank every month, and has a good laugh with the cashier.

I consider that I have experienced a rare opportunity. My diagnosis and illness have become simultaneously life-threatening and life-enhancing. The opportunity for evaluating one's life and one's purpose in life can be prompted by any number of events. None is more powerful than being told you are going to die soon. Perhaps it seems odd of me to refer to a terminal illness as an opportunity, yet that is precisely what I have done: viewed a seemingly hopeless situation as quite literally the chance of a lifetime. I have revitalized my goals and clarified my values. I feel satisfied with many aspects of my life. I have turned this deadly circumstance inside out. As the old adage goes, "If you have a lemon, make lemonade."

Don't think for a minute that the process of redefining my situation as a challenge is not gut-wrenching.
Every fiber in my being has been challenged by the
reality of my imminent death, my oh-so-human mortality. Yet, within the confines of a terminal illness,
indeed, the very confines of the mortal condition, there
are many choices and decisions that can be made. I
have made it my job to enhance the quality of my life.
My daily activities and social contacts have been limited. Relationships with my biological family have been
selective. Every moment deserves the consideration
and actualization of my life's desires. I certainly do
feel challenged.

You can make life closer to what you want it to be
by taking control of your health care. You can learn
to be responsible for your own health and responsive
to helping others with your needs. The first step is to
learn about your illness. If you are going to adapt in
a good way, you will have to get an objective grip on
your situation. *Keep* securing adequate information about
your illness. Then, you must do what you can to improve your life, while planning for your death. You
might want to keep a daily diary of symptoms, regulating your exercise, diet, and social interactions according to what you learn is best for you. Don't forget,
your doctor is at your side to help you coordinate your
health care.

When I want to achieve something, I set subgoals
that are short-term and consider specific means for
reaching those goals. I try to plan my day each morn-

ing, making lists of the things I am to do. This kind of approach to life lends itself to doing things that are good for me, because I feel committed to completing the tasks I plan.

I have coped by making efforts to manage, influence, change, or accept a particular problem. The fighting styles you select will depend in part on how you see your situation. Here several evaluations—like how much control you have over your illness, how life-changing it is, how much it was anticipated, and how long it will last—act together to determine your selection of a way to cope with a person, situation, or event. You can and should take responsibility for altering the course of your illness, however tiny or giant your goal. You must make a commitment to start somewhere. Even the most seemingly insignificant step can be the one that begins a path toward personal accomplishment. You should set goals that will support and strengthen your sense of purpose in life.

You will need to develop a quality of social support that you are satisfied with. Take the time to think through just what you do need from others. Social support is a complex concept, and not all so-called support is positive. For example, you may find that some want to rescue you from your problems, when, in fact, you feel the need to take charge of these problems yourself.

Say NO! to help that you feel is not helpful, but be prepared to help others help you. One way to do this is by telling them the truth: "Thank you, but I need to do this myself." I like doing my own food shopping when I am feeling up to it, so I often tell people who would do this for me that I would like to do it when I can, and I ask if I can pick up any items for them while I'm shopping. Talking openly with others about what I can and can't do helps us to divide tasks, sharing the caring. Some people will be more willing than others to talk openly, and genuinely to help out.

On the other hand, if you are lying in bed feeling oh-woe-is-me, you may generate pity in others. One disadvantage to the seeking of pity is the damage done to communications that results from the "pry it out of me" stance toward health care providers. Try to remember that in every loss there is something to regain—perhaps even to gain for the first time. Don't dwell on what you have lost. If you can't stand up to make your own bed, then get on all fours and make it. A lot of the hurdles you will face will seem insurmountable, but they are only impossible to overcome if you make them so.

Being persistent and self-confident under the pressure of a life-threatening illness is seen by others as an indication you won't die. "Ain't none of us going to make it out of this world alive," as the elderly gentleman in a vitamin store said to me, yet some people have remarked that I was too tough to die. Being a fighter has the disadvantage of sometimes making it seem to others that illness has special rewards. I have thought about the advantages and disadvantages of my illness a lot and have concluded that I would rather see the silver lining in the clouds another way. But I am sure of my own desires and this has helped me deal with others' reactions to my hardy coping. And excelling in our difficult circumstances has its own reward: superior survival followed by death with dignity.

Your daily strategies for coping should be common-sense ways to gain mastery over your life. Cancer and diseases of the internal organs, like renal failure, heart disease, and emphysema have many common symptoms. For example, many kinds of cancer are less bothersome than the side effects of treatment. People suffering from renal failure must deal with the disease and its treatment, particularly the stress of severe losses or restriction, such as reduced income, diminished sexual drive, changes in body image and appearance, impaired family activities, change of status in the family, reduced work competence, and reduced hopes for a good future. For each of us living with dying, we are apt to find ourselves adrift somewhere between the world of the sick and the world of the well, passionately involved in our struggle to work out realistic expectations and set reasonable goals.

Pain is another common factor. Your pain can be controlled in a number of ways, including: analgesics, minor tranquilizers, major tranquilizers, hypnotics and sedatives, stimulants, antidepressants or mood elevators, hallucinogens, muscle relaxants, anti-inflamatory agents and vasoactive compounds. There are also a lot of behavioral and psychological ways to cope with pain. A good source for tips on managing pain is *Coping with*

Chronic Pain, by Nelson Hendler and Judith Fenton (New York: Crown Publishers, Inc., 1979). This book has a very useful test for how much pain you have, and an excellent discussion of pain clinics and what they can do for you.

Other symptoms, such as skin problems, fever, and gastrointestinal problems may require specific treatment. Weakness and malaise are also common to many illnesses. You may need to schedule your activities around how much energy you feel like expending. You may have to apply special creams or wear special clothing before you go outside your house. But, as long as your ways of managing your health and illness are effective at controlling your symptoms, don't disrupt your social life, and are flexible to change, then your active participation in your total health care will create and maintain feelings of self-control. Perseverance supports the desire to survive and thrive. The belief and anticipation that you can be effective is self-motivating, and flexibility is helpful, because the daily hassles and crises of illness do require varied coping skills and strategies.

I decided to strike out on my own, taking charge of my medical care, after realizing the medical knowledge of my illness was limited. The greatest source of fear and anxiety I experienced was in *not knowing* what could be done to save my life. I did not know what symptoms the doctors could treat without exacerbating my underlying condition. I wondered what I could do to make myself as well and as satisfied with living as possible, for as long as possible. I demanded more information in order to make my own well-informed decisions.

I questioned how effective I could be, unless I could get the information I needed to make a reasonably informed decision. I did not know if I could implement the practical steps required to acquire information. I learned that collecting newspaper clippings about my illness was useful. I also read medical reports and journals related to cancer and to AIDS. In addition, I telephoned every hot line number I could get my hot little hands on. Often I doubted if I could handle what I might encounter if I did seek information about my illness. In fact, there were times when having a lot of information was overwhelming and negative. I had to use a medical dictionary a lot and found *Stedman's Medical Dictionary*, 24th Edition (Baltimore, Maryland: Williams & Wilkins, 1982) most helpful. Although I had to rely on friends and loved ones for hope when the medical information I received was convincingly fatalistic, I allowed myself to experience the intense emotions called forth, then I gathered the strength to move on.

I feared my independence and self-reliance would be misperceived by doctors as noncompliance, leading them to refuse to care for me when I needed them. This actually did happen on several occasions. One doctor called me "audacious" and another told me later that I appeared to some health care professionals "like an uppity black in the 1960s." But my perseverance helped me to find a supportive primary-care physician.

Lastly, I did not know how I would use what I learned. I should have realized that I am a natural helper, and that once I had learned how to apply my new knowledge to my own dilemma, I would be helping others. My efforts to unravel the mysteries of AIDS treatments became known to many others, and my telephone was soon ringing at all hours. A book I wrote to help others facing AIDS in America was published, and I designed a Stanford University study to implement my new cognitive-behavioral program for coping with AIDS. I would like to point out that this is my individual adaptation. Your own ways of adaptation must be especially tailored to your own personality and your needs.

Taking charge of my medical care was like any separation. The initial period of "striking out on my own" was filled overwhelmingly with intense anger, loss, and—ultimately—fear. The anger was because I felt I had relied on the Godlike image of doctors, only to be betrayed by their human limits. I resolved this by recalling some of my fellow undergraduates who went on to medical school. This helped me to accept the human limitations and potentials that join all of us in our mortal condition. Doctors are people, too.

At first, I felt at a loss when I decided not to consult doctors for every little thing that appeared problematic. I resisted the panicked message from within, "I need a doctor." Feelings of anxiety about whom to turn to for medical consultation and care consumed my thoughts. I took the time to get more familiar with what my body had to say. I took notice of the messages of fatigue and malaise and recorded them in a daily notebook. This was a good way to become more sensitive to my physical limits. I respected my physical reality, gave attention to my physical health, and started to gain control over my own wellness.

I began asking my primary-care physician to help me compile a list of symptoms and bodily functions to use as early warning signs requiring immediate medical attention, and an accompanying list of practical things I could do to control or moderate daily symptoms and bothersome events. I gained an understanding of how much and which symptoms I could control by developing an open communication with my care providers and seeking information on my own about health care alternatives. I understand the risks versus the benefits of various treatments. I learned that I can influence some symptoms and some of my reactions to the illness that threatens my life.

I do not feel like a backseat driver, but quite behind the wheel of my life. I don't know where the highway I travel along will lead all of the time, but I keep my eyes on the road and my hands on the wheel. Sometimes I feel like it doesn't matter what happens tomorrow, that all I have to do is live today. At other moments, I feel like I am living in the past with the present whizzing by me like signs along the expressway.

Time has a lot of importance in dealing with a life-threatening illness. I have noticed in conversations with friends and family that their preferences for time, past, present, or future, make them act in particular ways. Some people talk about the past like there is no today, wanting things to have been different in the past, or missing the good ol' days. If you place too much emphasis on the past, you might get trapped in feelings of blame or loss. This can lead to depression and withdrawal. Too much focus on the present may lead to risky behavior and not enough health-promoting acts. These people talk a lot about today being all we have. People in general are apt to make risky choices when facing situations in which their ability to manage the situation effectively is uncertain. Too much attention on the future can also create anxiety over uncertainty. Your goal should be to focus somewhat on planning ways to control immediate health matters.

Plan for living one day at a time, and you will be ready for the days to come. You don't have to be a person who lives in the past, hiding from the fate of the future. If you see yourself engaging in behaviors that are risky to your health, or not engaging in enough behaviors that will prolong your life by promoting your health, it may be because of your preference for the past. Don't get stuck in memories of a time gone by. It will only make the losses in your life since you became ill seem more important than they have to be. You can change that by reminding yourself that the present day as well as the days to come hold special things, too. Keeping a balanced sense of time will help you to cope by encouraging you to take positive actions. You can improve your health and happiness by effectively coping with the events in your daily living.

FOUR

HOPE AND REALISM:

Notes on Living Until We Say Goodbye

A lot of my friends, upon finding out about my illness, began to avoid me, apparently not knowing how to relate to me any longer, as though I were standing with one foot in the grave and the other on a banana peel. I think people's avoidance of the so-called "terminally ill" often represents their avoidance of thinking about death, but avoidance can also result from conflicts between a person's understanding of hope and realism, and a feeling that hope is a form of denial. What is hope? What is reality? What is denial? These questions are not as pleasing to us, perhaps, as the sweet-smelling rose of summer; yet, even the summer flowers spring from seeds in the dead of winter, and we, too, have our seasons.

I often feel like I am walking the line between getting

up and giving up. Yet, I seem to have a greater capacity for the truth now that I am among those living with dying. I have asked myself many times, "Am I crazy to be hopeful? Isn't reality telling me not to have hope? How can I live meaningfully among the people dear to me until we have to say goodbye? What can I expect?"

In myself and others I have seen the baneful effects of negative social beliefs about our life expectations. The expectations of individuals with AIDS are fueled by the beliefs about AIDS that are pervasive in our culture. Clearly most people believe that AIDS is fatal, striking down its victims and creating a sense of doom because there is no hope of controlling it. In addition, most people believe the available treatments are awful, producing many undesirable side effects. These social beliefs can have a devastating effect on one's morale. Newspapers and magazines often carry stories of people who have died following a long battle with cancer, heart disease, lung ailments, and most recently AIDS. The message delivered in these stories is usually how brave these people were; but the subtle message is that they were brave in the face of their inevitable death.

Just as fears of living and fears of dying are connected, the hopes of mortal beings stir conflict. I often sense in others a discomfort when I speak of my goals and activities. It is as though they are disturbed by an uncomfortable incompatability between the hope I feel and my acceptance of the inevitability of death.

To many people, hope in the face of a seemingly hopeless situation is acceptable only if it is based in religious faith and the grace of God. Ceremonial faith activities, like a pilgrimage to a special place, may create healthy hope by actively engaging the ill person in his or her well-being. Rituals can have this effect. Every year an estimated three million people make a pilgrimage to Lourdes, a place near the French Pyrenees, in hope of restoring their health. These people believe that the Virgin Mary appeared in 1858 to a French peasant girl, Marie Bernade Soubirous (Saint Bernadette). Nearby a spring was discovered at the very moment of the apparition, and since that event, millions of people have drunk from and bathed in the icy waters of the spring, and in doing so, taken an active role in their own well-being.

I think there are other ways for active faith to restore hope, hope that rejects death as an evil end to life. After all, we do all of us die. I have developed some rituals of hope of my own. At first, I planted garden vegetables that would take longer to harvest than I was supposed to live. I got to plant and reap the splendid harvests of several seasons' crops. And my cherry tomatoes yielded plenty for me and my friends. The bare and pale yellow cornstalks stood withered next to orange pumpkins and colorful gourds in the fall—for more than one fall! I was sort of challenging Mother Nature to a duel, with both sides agreeing that preserving life was our mutual purpose.

I selected a special place to go to for long walks alone. I had a very private spot on a beach. Facing the awesome power of an ocean wave, its white crest spraying to an endless horizon, helped me to place my life and my goals in a perspective I could live—and die—with.

The faith of religions places too much responsibility in the hands of some unclear external authority to suit me. My faith is also in the human potential. I have seen too many friends die with their faith in God intact, while their daily activities to promote their own well-being diminished. Faith healing can be fatal. I am participating in my own health and death care, while personally disengaging from some people, places, and things in my life. My faith is in some greater world, incomprehensibly civilized. It is a world beyond me, but one I can trust.

I found a unique kind of hope in the months immediately following my diagnosis. I was already growing toward a hope that was as great as the highly evolved society I had envisioned. I was often alone in my hopefulness. I could sense from others a lack of confidence that revealed more despair in them than I felt myself. Odd, I thought. Yet, I was keenly aware of how they communicated their hopelessness. For example, one of my physicians, previously an understanding expert with ready answers, attempted to become a philosopher by comforting me with trite remarks after I was diagnosed with cancer and AIDS. The most profound communication from this doctor was his avoidance of my questions. I sensed his "cave of despair" attitude through both anxious and awkward verbal, and tense nonverbal, cues. The message was clear: I would not survive, and my remaining life would be awful.

My experience has shown me that many terminally ill people have been capable of achieving the courage and strength to change their negative beliefs about living with dying. Many people grow to understand that even if they can't totally recover, they can have rewarding times. They still have to muster the courage to resolve their own fears about their illness, while coping with the negative expectations of the people around them.

This method of assessing your beliefs and expectations is a regrouping task, requiring that you adapt your beliefs in a way that produces the optimal amount of healthy survival possible. Actively diminish the negative expectations about medical treatment for your illness with the positive thought that medical treatment can be an important ally. It is possible and desirable to integrate your health and your illness. You can reach a compromise in your way of living that allows for, but does not bow to, your illness. Try to keep an open mind as you are interpreting what your illness means to your life, leaving room for a banana split or the viewing of a funny film.

Don't get down on yourself if you experience difficulty in persuading yourself to change your beliefs from negative to positive. Perhaps you have had negative experiences that "prove" the validity of your negative beliefs about life-threatening illness and death. You don't have to diminish your past experiences in order to hope for something better. The point I want to make is that you should gain from the knowledge you learned the first time around! Your primary goal here is to make sure your expectations are working for you rather than against you. You can keep your morale working for you by pinning your hope to the sunny side of things!

The first step in changing your negative expectations is to become aware of what you do believe. Then you can see more clearly the potential effects of your beliefs about living until you have to say goodbye. The next steps involve setting specific goals that keep you connected to living.

Try describing what you believe about your illness into a tape recorder sometime. Respond to the question: "What do you believe about medical treatments for your illness?" Then take about five minutes to describe how you feel about your future with the illness. Last, replay the tape. Listen to the tone and speed of speech in the tape-recorded voice. Listen to both *what* and *how* you speak.

- Do you sound angry, sad, or what?

- Do you pause and stammer when you speak about things that make you anxious?

- How intense do you sound?

- Are the emotions you are expressing familiar to you?

- How negative or displeasing to you are the things you hear?

This exercise has helped me in the way it helps me to write letters that are never sent: I get acquainted with myself. After doing the voice recording, I was able to see how many of my decisions were being shaped by a limited view of what was possible for me to do and be.

At this point the question of false hope entered for me. I knew that my positive attitude would not guarantee recovery, but I also believed I could establish a healthy dose of reasonable hope. The notion of false hope suggests that people should never have hope as long as there is a reason to believe that they will be disappointed. But the fear of having false hope undermines our foundation for living a full life. It can prevent healthy adaptations for dealing with a threat to life by dashing one's hopes. Similarly, I enter my personal relationships with no guarantee that they will be happy and fulfilling. I generally try to approach people with the expectation that our relationship will probably be a good one. This does not always produce successful relationships, but I believe it gives them a chance. On the other hand, I have had times when, mostly due to an overall crisis in faith or trust, I entered with the expectation a relationship would fail, and it usually did under those negative anticipations. "Be not afraid of life. Believe that life is worth living and your belief will help create the fact," said William James.

I have worked hard to develop and apply my approach to my life-threatening illness, yet I know I will indubitably face death. I have significantly outlived my prognosis by several years. I have lived a more rewarding life than I would have had I not actively participated in my wellness.

Is not death inevitable for us all? My advice is to confront the possibility of death openly. *Death is not failure.* Living under the excuse of self-imposed limitations might be considered failure, though. *A diagnosis is an event to be adapted to, not a death sentence to be compliant with!*

Hope and acceptance of death are the same in many respects. By enjoying the moment we affirm our life with the recognition of our ultimate mortality. The people to whom you are attached will remind you that you are still the same person with all of the same life experiences you had before you became ill. Talk about all the topics, issues, or people you previously spoke about with your friends. Make special appointment times to see familiar faces, and keep your commitment to those dates. Being in familiar places helps by grounding your experience in your own personal world. I have found that it is not enough to take time out to smell the roses—it's more assuring and effective to grow your own roses to smell!

A very important emotional theme that you may experience is an overwhelming sense of loss in your own life's purpose. This feeling of purposelessness can become an utter despair that seems to drive one to die. Ask yourself why you are feeling such despair about your purpose in life. Keeping an open and active mind builds your power to generate choices. Admittedly, some of your choices will be shaped by physical limitations and some will be determined by social attitudes toward your illness. The important element, in both creating and carrying out choices that enhance your purposefulness, is to resist imposing false limitations on your potential. This is a tough task for you as an individual, and even more difficult for institutions you might want to be involved with. You must strike a balance between the real and the not-so-real, understanding that you can do some meaningful things. Reject opportunities from social organizations or institutions that would provide a structure for regulating your stigma, rather than promoting your success. Very few common institutions (family, church, state, and school) have truly enfranchised the terminally ill. Limit your choices for activities when they impose negative limits on you. If you perceive yourself as having the power of choice, you will live longer than those who do not!

Thucydides provides a powerful example in his book *History of the Peloponnesian War*. He became ill with a plague in 430 B.C., but recovered and became a general. He writes, "The most terrible thing of all was the despair into which people fell when they realized that they had caught the plague: for they would immediately adopt an attitude of utter helplessness, and, by giving in this way, would lose their powers of resistance."

I have discovered that one of the most important feelings to have is a satisfaction with life and self-image. I want to be alive! My life has a great deal of meaning to me, and I can see how much I mean to others. I frequently do things I enjoy, and I feel in good spirits most of the time. I enjoy a gradual lessening of anxiety about death. I also feel an increasing sense of spiritual satisfaction.

When others are concerned about false hope they often see themselves as realists. They may take pride in seeing life as it really is. But this view blocks out hope. It is not realism but pessimism. Such an approach to living may protect one from disappointment, but it can also create negative limitations on choice that produce ill effects on the individual facing the life-threatening illness.

Others may express concern and talk of false hope as though you were engaged in some form of quackery. When this happens to me, I admit that it is true that there are a number of nontraditional approaches to life-threatening illness that do not appear to have a scientific basis. I remind skeptics that it is not always easy to make definitive judgments about the worth of such approaches. I simply acknowledge that we do not know if recoveries are really occurring as a result of treatments, or as a result of the person's belief in the treatment. But who cares? Realistically speaking, do what works for you and hope for the best! Even entering the inner sanctum of the hospital, going through tests and examinations, may provide a ritualistic benefit. The very act of going to the doctor is a response to a mental, albeit biologically prompted, message. And some people feel better after just going to the doctor.

Native Americans believe in healers. The shaman healers among the Native Americans offer both a remedy and a ritual to their ill. In these rituals, the rich lore of ceremony is shared in events that involve the participation of the entire family. The healer focuses on others' reactions to the illness, rather than the illness per se. The healer works with the patient to establish an agreement about what the the illness means. And in the end, as a man with AIDS noted, "They get their tribe together and participate with you." Dying is a community event akin to a celebration, the celebration of a life together.

Let's be absolutely clear on this point: Medical science can't account for the extraordinary degree to which belief can affect the outcome of life-threatening illness. Our focus must remain on the power of our beliefs. I started changing negative beliefs by simply becoming aware of the manner by which beliefs affect outcomes in many areas of my daily life. I did this by keeping a journal in which I logged the feelings I had before meeting a new person, and the outcome of the encounter after I returned from it. Journal entries would begin with sentences such as, "I feel like this person could be trusted." I focused on my personal "buttons," those ultrasensitive areas I have in my character. And I found that I really dislike being dependent and helpless, so I work very hard to be self-reliant.

Once I began to see how belief helps create experience, I found it easier to apply that concept to my illness and use it to achieve well-being. Now, I think

I can moderate my physical and psychic energy, encouraging attempts that have a positive influence on my health. By believing in my ability to titrate to life, I am creative and influence my well-being. These are the important elements in my basic operating morale. I have made deliberate efforts to acquire positive beliefs about my ability to have a positive impact on my life and death. I encourage my recognition of the fact that I can change the way I see things. And by exposing myself to these processes and ideas I have become sensitive to alternative ways of viewing life, and death. Now I can see when I am responsible for a turn of events and when I am not. I have learned that there are some conflicts that cannot be resolved to my satisfaction, and when they are not, I can effectively bury the hatchet. I have learned the value of a "short turnaround," doing what gets a quick reward. I have learned that enjoying the moment is worth it.

Your outlook for the future will determine your ability to hang in there. It can enable you to develop and maintain reasonably high goals. Your basic objective should be the planning of your next action within the realistic limits of what is possible. Your goals can now be tempered by your realistic expectations for the future, and enhanced by your wishes and your daydreams. This approach will ensure that your goals will be determined by your personal values, and your sense of realism in regard to the probability of reaching the goal. You may have a private timetable, one that predicts how long you *really* expect to survive. Probe your expectations about how many more days you will live. The goal in exploring your survival timetable is to gain awareness of how to use it to satisfy the quality of your life. One of the benefits of this awareness is that once you come to terms with what is real and not-so-real about your diagnosis, you can turn your attention to coping with living.

Keep your ambition down to earth. Set your goals so as to enjoy living while you are surviving. You can keep in touch with your biological reality and determine your own productivity and morale. Focusing on the quality of living and dying with your values in alignment will encourage you to still have goals. Steadily aspire to illuminate the values and purposes that your life has stood for.

I do not feel that to accept death is to surrender. I now understand that hope in the face of death is *not* denial. This acceptance of death without denial prevents me from giving up all resistance, which would lead me to simply acquiesce. I hope to exert some degree of influence on the events surrounding me. I certainly do desire survival, but I don't have to have absolute control in order to have authentic hope. I may be feeling finite, but I am not feeling futile!

Even though many of the dying people I have met are often without hope, a shortened life does not in itself create hopelessness. People lose hope when they are unable to act on their own behalf and must give up their connections with important people in their lives. Hoping is a healthy act of living, and death is a dimension of living. Merely to survive is hardly worth the price for those who are being kept alive only because of external artificial support. In these cases, it is not that the person no longer wants to stay alive, but rather that survival is no longer necessary. Authentic hope is nourished by a healthy respect for dying. Hope can naturally accompany the acceptance of death.

Sometimes I feel that I need healthy people more than they need me. But this is not always true. The living need the dying as the dying need the living. We remind one another that if we accept being alive, then we must also accept the fact of death. When I connect with others in ways that are positive in the face of death and dying, I try to let them know how good it makes me feel by sending a simple thank-you note, or a letter.

Hope is an important element of survival for us. The hope we need, though, is essentially a positive attitude toward life. One kind of hope can be learned, by producing one's sense of optimism and expectation by means of recollections of past successes. You can augment hope by thinking of several successful examples of prior events you have coped with. Make a list of the toughest times in your life and recall how you coped in the crises that turned out okay. What does it take for you to get through tough times? Don't forget to be your own best cheerleader!

Talk to others about their hope. When you feel hopeless, others can often empower you by sharing their own experiences. Hope is an elusive sentiment. Yet hope remains important in sustaining life. The healing power of hope has been reported in numerous cases, and it is just as clear that people do die sooner than they might otherwise if they have no hope. The news is full of stories that tell of people who defy medical odds to satisfy some important reason to be alive. Hope, like love, is balm for the mortal's plight.

In his book *Hope* (New York: Bruner/Mazel Publishers), Arnold A. Hutschnecker reports a study of two hundred patients, each of whom maintain at least a little hope, explaining that people without hope see no end to their suffering but those with hope have confidence in the desirability of survival. "It's true," author and cancer patient N. D. Spingarn says, "hope gives us hanging in [there] patients something to live for, it enables us to endure uncomfortable tests and tedious treatments."

This is more than a matter of survival, it is a matter of the quality of *how* we live and die. We must redefine our stance toward our experience with life-threatening disease so that there is room for hope. We must also strive to reach an agreement with others about what hope means to us. You can view your death as the ultimate achievement in a life of preparedness. You can exit life in your own style, just as you have lived in your own style. Your values will remain and ensure your sense of integrity. Your enhanced capacity for the truth will guide you to it. *Hope and realism are not*

opposites, they are not incompatible. We can be prepared for dying while planning for living as we can be
prepared for living while planning for dying. In our
growing understanding and upsurging wisdom, a strange
and wonderful paradox is revealed:

Hope grows from the soil of human mortality.

FIVE

TAKING STOCK OF YOUR LIFE:

Working Through Events and Relationships While Caring for Yourself

Taking stock of the major events in your life and your most satisfying friendships is reminiscent of the Christmas carol about Santa making a list and checking it twice. Making a list of the important people and events in your life is a useful step toward understanding "what makes you tick." It involves remembering the deepest, most heartfelt times of your life. You will be stronger in the days ahead if you have at your fingertips the lessons of days gone by.

Taking stock is not a simple phase, or a temporary state of mind. More than simply remembering, taking stock of your life involves thinking about it, judging parts of it, and affirming parts of it. It is a process of assessing values, decisions, and goals, and then of reassessing them as new insights emerge.

Taking an inventory of your life will awaken your memory and clarify the values that have contributed to the quality and purpose of your life. You can take stock of what you value by describing the things you like and dislike about work, friends, family members, or religion. Perhaps one of the most useful results of this deliberate extension of thought to the past will be an affirmation of who you are, coupled with an appreciation of how you came to be.

Start by asking yourself if you are really getting what you want out of life. Make a list of twenty things in life that you love to do. Then look at each of the items to see which require money, planning, being with other people or being alone, and which ones you would not have listed five years ago. Rank the five most important items, number one being the thing you most love to do. You may want to consider how much risk the activity has to you physically, emotionally, or intellectually. Can you do the things you most love at any time of the year? Are some of the things you love to do more conventional than others?

According to Jerry Weinstein of the Center for Humanistic Education, University of Massachusetts, you can use this exercise to crystallize new learning by completing these sentences:

- I learned that . . .

- I realized that . . .

- I noticed that . . .

- I was surprised that I . . .

- I was pleased that I . . .

- I was displeased that I . . .

With the information you gain from taking stock, you can move toward acting on your values. Start by answering the question: "Am I really doing what I want with my life?" To help you answer that question and act on it, authors Sidney Simon, Leland Howe, and Howard Kirschenbaum give the following advice in their book, *Values Clarification* (New York: Hart Publishing Company, 1972): First, prepare a paper with three columns, including "What I'd like to learn or do or be able to do better" in column one; put the date you want to start your actions in column two; and in column three, write out the first step you will take. Topics in column one might include relating to other people, having fun, a particular hobby, and how you deal with your illness. Your starting date should be based on a realistic plan that considers your health and your resources. The plan of action you begin will be based on a genuine desire that you have clarified, so your motivation will create its own momentum. You will need to consider how to put your plan in action, and it can be particularly useful to talk with a friend at this point. If intimacy is one of the things you would like to get better at, this will be a natural step. Whatever your values and goals, this exercise can help clarify them for you, putting your motive in motion.

You may find it useful to sketch out your autobiography. This will help you to examine the patterns in certain events in your past. For example, list the people who have taught you valuable lessons about life, or have been otherwise influential in your learning, such as teachers or parents. According to the authors of *Values Clarification*, you might benefit from writing down each major turning point in your life, starting with the earliest age you can recall. How did they occur? How did they make you feel then, and how do they make you feel now? In addition, make a list of the best friends you have had in your life. Write about the activities you enjoyed together and what you liked about the person. Notice who your best friends are now, and discover the similarities and differences between your past and present friendships.

Other questions to pose to yourself include:

- What have been the happiest times during the past year? And the unhappiest?

- What are the greatest achievements in your life?

- What occupations have you wanted to be involved in since you finished high school? Describe what appeals to you about each job.

You will most likely need to assess your employment situation after receiving a terminal diagnosis. It seems that each of us has some internal clock of living/dying that springs from our deepest goals and aspirations. The commitment you have to your career, and to your very physical relationship to the material world, does not diminish readily. The frustrations you feel at having goals blocked can generate intense anger. Don't be alarmed at this. The goal of taking stock in regard to work is to be happy with what you are going to do about it. Ask yourself, what gives me a sense of purpose? When do I feel the most valued? List as many options as you and your care partner can think of that would fulfill your needs regarding employment and purposefulness. Earning money for your efforts may or may not be as important now as it was before diagnosis. Be open to such changes in your values, using them to think of alternatives like volunteer work. You may find that you need to take time to satisfy these special needs.

It is important that you develop your own plan or strategy for doing what you value and desire. Take the time to consider what you liked about prior jobs, what hobbies or talents you have, and what objective limits your current situation imposes. Then make a plan for living the remainder of your life that will contribute to your sense of purposefulness.

Taking stock of my life and my important activities led me to examine my satisfaction with work. Previously, about one year before my diagnosis, I was a manager for a hi-tech personnel company. Then, I had accepted a job as manager for a large apartment complex in a multi-ethnic neighborhood. My protective managerial style was well suited to community living. This was the most round-the-clock stress-inducing job I had ever held. I was a very good resident manager, management consultant, and laborer. Yet I was staying up at nights, writing my first book. My true passion for life was realized most when I was writing, and I couldn't stay away from it.

I was content with the work I had at the time of my diagnosis. I had just taken a job at Stanford University that would allow me to develop my skills in social psychology, as the Foreign Student Advisor at the Bechtal International Center on campus. In the beginning, I was under a lot of pressure to learn about the experiences of people from other cultures and to master the seemingly ever-changing Immigration and Naturalization Service regulations.

Taking stock of my prior job satisfaction helped me to decide how to spend my time. I grew to see what made life meaningful to me. I felt happiest when I was writing. My values became clearer regarding a number of matters: the acquisition of money, making a contribution to society, getting close to people I cared for, and caring for myself. Now I tend to get involved in activities that correspond with my expectations of how long I hope to survive as a functioning person. I even wrote my own autobiography, obituary, and tombstone inscription, just to see if I was doing what I valued, and to see what I might want to change while I still could. I suggest writing one page in response to each of the important questions facing you, such as:

- Why do you want to be alive?

- How long do you expect to be alive?

- What are your most important values now that you have been diagnosed?

- How do you want to be remembered?

- How can you best take an active role in possible hospitalizations?

- Whom do you want to feel closest to when you die?

Up to now, you may have been happy with working extra hours to get ahead in your career, but a change in your values about work can lead you to new choices. Make a list of your favorite activities and people, and schedule events and appointments for the upcoming weeks.

My motivation to work as long as I am physically able is viewed by others with mixed emotions. Some people seem to believe that the value of an ill person's work is less than that of a healthy person. Others use words like "return on investment," when speaking about scholarships for people with terminal illnesses. And, unfortunately, I have also been exploited and lied to by representatives of institutions and social-service agencies in order to gain my endorsement, or to gain public acclaim for themselves. I have found it necessary to take care that others do not take advantage of me during this time of vulnerability. It helps me to ask my closest confidant to comment on situations that are hard for me to be objective about.

Taking stock of your past relationships will bring memories that reflect the satisfaction you have felt with intimacy. It is important to recall the people who were pleasant. Such fond memories help us to cling tighter to the qualities we seek and admire in others. Yet, when we carry our thoughts back, the view will not always be pretty. Some people and events will have to be "pulled by the sleeve" to be remembered. Others will flash clearly across the mind. Be prepared for your imagination to put you in "a fine frenzy."

The shock of diagnosis passed, and I eventually set out to take stock of my past life by examining the most significant events in it and my friendships. I started this process by writing down several of the major events of my life, making a list, then recalling their details on tape. I talked freely into my little pocket-sized tape recorder. Later, I actually transcribed some of what I had said, while I erased the rest forever. Simply listening to myself talk about my life and my friendships was a learning experience. I began to harness the know-how I had already acquired.

In this way you often learn how the feelings you have today are shaped by the events of yesterday. The feelings and beliefs you have about your illness and what it will cause you to need from others are fertile grounds to start from, for they are apt to bring forth insights about yourself. Several other topics to look back at include: past experiences with being ill, past experiences with needing physical help, past experiences with trust, past sources of self-worth, and the present feelings you have regarding your own worth. Take the time to reflect on your growing-up years. In old age, dying people often take time to reminisce about how worthwhile and sensible their life was. Many old people are not "ready" to die until they have made a certain peace within themselves.

The process of looking back is one way to affirm that your life has been valuable. You can see that you have done the best that you could when possible. You may even discover that you know a lot more about how to handle this illness experience than you initially thought.

My own life inventory exercises led me to recall some family experiences that were very satisfying. I had visited my grandparents on my father's side frequently as a child. I recall how I used to stand unnoticed in the doorway of my grandfather's old log milk barn and watch him perform a task he had done for over sixty years. The massive, sluggish German would let his milk cow into the barn, where feed awaited her. He squatted heavily on the tiny brown wooden milkstool, taking his usual position at the fawn-colored flank. Speaking softly to her, his thick hands gently massaged the cow's udder as the pail filled with streams of fresh white milk. Hungry cats stood by awaiting their share of the foamy food. The cow instinctively munched her feed. The suspenders of Grandfather's wilted blue overalls drooped on his shoulders, which were slumped from age. Slowly, maturity had threatened him with baldness, leaving him now with only a trimming of thin gray hair around his ears and back of his head. As the sun set, a ray of light shone through a crack in the timeworn logs, revealing the deep wrinkles in his weathered face. Lifting the brimming pail of milk in one hand as the other helped to steady his stiff back, he slowly, painfully straightened up, leaving the cow to finish her feed.

It was important for me to retrieve the memory of my grandfather because I could not be near him. Even though I will never again feel the satisfaction of his company, I feel content with my images of him. Similarly, I had special places in my past to remember, especially a secret place of retreat that I named "The Crystal Cave."

The Crystal Cave was located about one hundred steps up a hill from a fence of rocks. A most unique characteristic of the cave was its entrance. It was a hole about three feet wide; you could not see the bottom, only knarled roots reaching downward into the dark. I had to slide down a fifteen-foot leaf-covered and snake-ridden tunnel that opened up to a room of about ten by fifteen feet with a ceiling eight feet high. In the first room of the cave there were wall carvings dating from the early 1800s, and bones of animals dragged there by the black panthers that were said to stalk the Ozark Mountain region.

Making my way carefully through the cavern's many twists and turns, eventually, I would end up in another room. This one also had dates and names carved into the walls as far back as the early 1800s, but fewer. Little brown bats hung from the ceiling and occasionally darted about my head. The stalactites that dripped from the ceiling and the stalagmites that projected upward from the floor of the cavern sparkled in the reflections of the carbon light beaming from my cap.

The next tunnel was a real challenge! The cave's crystal room was in the very back. It was about eight feet long with a one-and-a-half-foot ceiling and a stream in its muddy floor. On the other side was the secret to life itself for me.

I used to retreat to the crystal cave at least once a month with a box of birthday candles in my pocket. After sliding out of the muddy tunnel, the cave plunged downward another twenty feet to a small stream with salamanders in it. The tiny rocks covering the bottom of the stream looked polished. On the other side of the stream the cave sloped upward eight or ten feet. A shelf of sorts had formed in one corner of the rather large room. On one wall of the shelf, the crystal formations reaching downward met gently with the upreaching ones, blending into a smooth surface of transparent crystal. The crystal cave earned its name by this prismatic view through a sheet of earth. I would use the carbon light on my cap to take handfuls of the red clay from the tiny stream, then roll the clay into little sticky balls. I stuck a candle in each one and put the clay mounds onto the crystal wall.

There I felt at peace with life and the earth. It seemed the light of the crystal cave was permeating my very soul. A sense of self-sufficiency developed. I grew to appreciate life on earth. I believed I could survive whatever was dealt to me as I sat in the glow of the crystal cave survival lights. I could survive, I could stay alive. I felt a part of the marvelous earth. It seemed I could see into the earth. The world and its meaning to me became as transparent as the crystal itself. It even sparkled!

These memories helped me claim my prior experiences with life in a way that made postdiagnosis survival more desirable and more possible.

It is important to point out that focusing attention on pent-up feelings can be negative. You will need to limit how much you let your dwelling on the past influence your daily mood and experience. The general guideline I use is that I stop the remembering or "working through" process when it weakens me to the point of exhaustion. I listen to my body for signs of stress, like tenseness and tiredness. I stop and relax, bringing my focus in to the moment. Otherwise, taking stock would feel negative, like "raking up the past," instead of harvesting it. It is true that some memories are tucked away in the corners of our mind because they would haunt us if released. The goal you should work toward as you take stock of negative and unresolved thoughts of the past is to use them constructively by expressing and resolving emotions.

A useful tool in looking at life and resolving old relationships is the unsent letter. Learning happens when the link is made between what you feel and what is actually happening. You can write a lot of unsent letters to people to whom you have something to say. These letters may be words you wanted to speak, or conversations you wanted to have. It does not matter that it might be futile to send them, or that some of the people you address are already dead.

Writing letters to lost loved ones can help us lift a heavy emotional burden. Charles Bissell writes the following in his book, *Letters I Never Wrote, Conversations I Never Had* (New York: Macmillan Publishing Company, 1983):

> After the first letter I was exhausted. Lancing a wound can leave you reeling. Yet, after a few minutes, my breathing was deep and more relaxed than I have ever experienced. It was as if an anvil had been lifted off my chest—an unnecessary burden I had carried for years . . . . Another benefit has been to look at the reality of death. Death is

inevitable, but I am not powerless. I have the ability to decide how I will use my life. The choice is mine. I can hide or come out and play.

You can acknowledge when your sadness is valid and needs to be expressed. Move with it. Learn by looking at your past and use your depression as a signal to change what is bothering you!

Taking stock of the past will naturally lead you to examine your present relationships. The most demanding issue in coping with terminal illness and dying in the middle of one's life involves one's relationships with others. The prospect of leaving loved ones and of not fulfilling your relationships to others can be a major source of difficulty. Feelings of guilt for abandoning loved ones are common. You may sense your life is failing, and fear the loss of all control.

You may find yourself caught between planning for your loved ones and grieving your anticipated loss of them. It has been useful for me to realize that I can encourage the people I love to live a full and happy life. Set aside time to think about each person you feel you are leaving in some sense. Look at what you hope their life will hold and celebrate their future. You might do some special thing for a loved one on *your* birthday. For example, I was feeling a bit down on my birthday recently, thinking about how many more birthdays I would have. I stopped dwelling on that thought, and attended a flute recital at which my lover was performing. His career as a flutist may not reach its peak during my life, but that doesn't preclude my support and participation *now*. There were special arrangements I had to make in order to stay for the entire performance, but knowing my birthday was a gift affirming the life of a loved one was worth a lot.

The areas of satisfaction I looked at led me to talk openly about what gives me enjoyment. I have discovered that taking time to be happy for others helps me feel less sad about my missing out. I also permit myself to be angry about my circumstance, but not mad at the world for letting me down. In this way, I have prevented a crisis in my faith of a fair and just world.

When my lover first saw this chapter, he said, "You should stop and consider what I'm going through."

"Oops," I mumbled to myself. I was a little embarrassed that he felt my process of assessment was neglecting him. But his point was well taken.

"What *are* you feeling?" I asked him.

"Well, at first," he began, "when you told me the results of the lesion biopsy, all I could do was cry and hold you. After that, I jumped into an automatic mode of saying there would not be any problem, you would be healed and there was no reason for worry. I guess that was denial that you have a life-threatening illness. Since I have faced the truth, or is it the mystery, of the illness, I have had strange swings in moods. First,

I get angry at thinking the whole thing doesn't feel fair. Then I feel a strong sense of hope, like that someone will find a cure in time to help you. It's still hard to believe, because you look so healthy, but the tumor is always there to remind me. Sometimes I feel deep despair and fright, and I wonder, what will I do without you?"

During the next few hours, I learned that I was not alone in my awkwardness about making plans. The spouse or loved one caring for a person with a terminal diagnosis may often feel guilty about planning ahead. They may feel like planning ahead is betraying you by leaving you behind. And, there is another kind of guilt: Guilt because they are healthy.

The fact that I am satisfied with the love I receive from the person closest to me has been vital to my effective coping. This is an especially important consideration for people who are living with dying: How do we feel about the primary person in our life? Your most significant other may be a husband, wife, lover, or best friend. You will be evaluating the amount of satisfaction that you obtain from your primary friendship a lot during the period of taking stock after diagnosis.

There are many ways a couple can work together to manage the changes a terminal diagnosis has on each member, and on the couple. One way involves setting short-term goals that can be planned and achieved by both people. A couple can make sure that these short-term goals support mutually held long-term goals. In addition, each person in the couple must be prepared to face a life without the other's constant companionship. Some of this preparation will need to be done together, and some will require individual efforts to talk with others. Each person must be open and honest about what feelings emerge for him or her. After all, each must face daily health crises and hassles individually.

I have become sensitive to the times when the people closest to me need to know that it's okay to leave me alone. My reaction to others can make the difference between their feeling guilty for not spending every breathing moment with me and their feeling that the times we spend together are blessed by their other activities and friendships. I do tell them when I need to have company. I consider that if the person is brave and loving enough to help me face death, he deserves my encouragement to face his own life.

If you have children, there will be several special considerations for you to make. Depending on the changes brought about by your particular diagnosis, and the needs of your children, you will be making some difficult decisions. After all, your children may have to consider ways to talk with you about your illness as much as you have to consider ways to approach them on the issue. They may tell you of your diagnosis, or you may tell them of it. Either way, the golden rule of caring for each other is the same: Let the person talking set the tone and depth of the conversation while listening carefully!

The responsibilities you have to your children must and can be handled in a way that leaves the children strong enough to live their own lives. The rules for telling others about your illness vary according to certain primary concerns, such as the effects of stigma. However, a young child is hardly going to react (initially) with moral disdain at the prospect of losing a parent. If your child or children are not independent they may feel unimaginably alone and abandoned after your death.

If you decide not to tell your children that you are dying, you should take special steps lest their feelings of being betrayed or forsaken become a greater problem than their grief. Here's what to do if your children must be cared for away from home: First, make arrangements with the person you want to take care of your child or children to do so. How you and your spouse select the parent-elect will be a highly personal and deeply emotional task. You may want to begin this process as soon as possible, consulting an attorney for legal advice on trusts and guardianship. Then, instruct this person(s) that they are to assure your child or children that you died quietly and in peace, that now you will not have any pain—but that they will not have you with them anymore.

The parent-elect should tell your child or children whatever you want them to, including that you love them always, that so-and-so will take care of them, and that they are not alone. "How Children View Death," a chapter written by David Carroll (*Living with Dying*), contains excellent pointers regarding the things to say or do with a child when a close relative has died. It helps to educate children properly concerning death, and Carroll describes several good ways of going about it.

There are more mundane and concrete items to consider if you are a parent. Many of these issues are legal, and should be discussed with a legal expert. You can still take care of many of the provisions for your child or children that you dreamed of. Your will can allow for a college trust fund, if that is what you desire. Discuss with them the details that are important to you. For example, even if you can't make it to a child's college graduation, you can plan now to make a gift that can be delivered by another. The confidence in your preparedness will strengthen those you are departing from, giving the greatest gift of all: They will know they were loved.

You will need to take stock of your family and how they will be influenced by your illness. Depending on your primary role responsibilities, your absence will have different implications. It will be necessary to think about what you can honestly expect from your family ties. Then, the ways your family will be changed by your illness and death can be determined. Some of your most important remaining decisions will evolve from the resolutions you make about your family. This is true regardless of the kind of relationship you have had with them in the past.

Taking stock of your family at this time of your life is important because it can make your dying and their living more or less satisfactory. Most importantly, your life now and in the upcoming days can be molded by you, if you are quick to shape your social support network. Focus on the issues that are important to you, like your feelings about accepting financial support, special attention, et cetera.

Family relationships have a way of becoming transparent under the stress and strain of a life-threatening illness. Family can sometimes be so unsupportive that complete exclusion is required. This is relatively rare, however. Under the stress of a death most people experience a closer bonding with the other members of their family. This is a time for all involved to keep in mind that we only get one biological family.

The changes in the family that are prompted by your illness should be handled with honest conversation. These changes may involve who makes important decisions in your absence. The amount of time you can spend doing the activities you used to do may diminish as your illness causes physical limitations. Yet the stress and strain your family may feel from pressing needs caused by your illness can be effectively managed. Here are several things to do:

- Talk with the family members involved in your daily care about the amount of time each person has available to care for you.

- Divide up the tasks among your family members as they make themselves available.

- Express your concern for the loved ones who give so much time and energy that they suffer fatigue and strain.

- Involve the people you want to involve in this time of your life.

If some family members are not particularly welcome in your hospital room, you should tell them so. Compassion isn't always possible or authentic for some people, and this is no time to pretend.

Don't expect your disconcerted family members to tolerate more than they normally do. For example, if you are feeling angry about dying, you might vent your anger rather thoughtlessly and even aimlessly toward those closest to you. Some family members will remain confronting and challenging, while others will not. Often the loved ones of dying people are taught to "grin and bear it." However, it may be more adaptive to have the family members remain as tolerant or nontolerant as before.

There are no hard and fast rules about how to be with your family under your particular circumstance. But, as much as possible, be who you have always been and allow others to retain their personalities. Particular symptoms may require special physical and social arrangements, so try to keep an open mind to the ways your family will need to change in response to your illness. This can be a time for you to participate in helping your family adapt to the reality of being without you. By facing this harsh reality together, your family can become stronger. Some of the other benefits to you of having your family's support may include that you will live longer and with more gusto than you would without their support. The benefits to your family of having their support and care accepted by you may include that they, too, will live longer and happier lives than if you had refused their affection.

I have heightened my awareness of what I need and want in my intimate friendships by looking at times in the past. In my recollections of old relationships, several important lessons about friendship emerged. Now I apply those lessons to my current friendships. For example, I remember how valuable support for career goals can be. Many of my same-age friends are looking forward to a planned career. By supporting their potential, I hope to be remembered when their successes are celebrated.

A critical first step in meeting your responsibilities to friends is to hold on to your own sense of self-worth. Consider how you want to be thought of, the images you want your name to draw forth. Consider also that your lesson in death and dying can be shared honestly. *Our first responsibility to others is to be with them while we can be.* Ironically, our first responsibility to ourselves is also to find the value in being still alive. The message you will impart to your loved ones by dying with your self-esteem intact will leave them facing life courageously.

Taking stock of my life gave me good things to say about who I am and what my abilities are, such as:

- I know I am a good person, that I deserve to live, and that I am strong enough to get through today.

- I have mastered difficult situations before.

- If others think me unfriendly, I remind myself that I am friendly, generous, and thoughtful.

- I do not deserve ill treatment from anyone.

- I am not helpless and I do not have to be lonely.

- I am intrinsically a fighter!

Also, I consider each negative statement about myself worth one point, and each positive one to be worth ten points, if anyone is counting. So, it takes a lot of negative statements to overwhelm just a few mighty strengths. This is more than simply a counterbalance of the negative messages about my illness with positive beliefs. My positive statements also serve me by supporting a basic attitude that says I am effective at influencing my own survival. Survival is desirable and my ability to influence it is locked in place. My strategies have proven themselves by my extended survival.

Taking stock of the past, while taking care of yourself today, may show you a view of life that you have not yet seen. That view can contain a clear picture of your values in comparison with the values reflected by your community, friends, and family. You can appreciate how you saw yourself and others in the past.

It is often helpful to examine what you expected of others and how you reacted as a child. You will discover your own satisfactions and realizations as you look back on your life. For example, having a sense of what you feel you missed out on in childhood can enable you to create it in your life now, if you haven't already done so. Try to see the special skills you developed in your childhood, not only the losses you may have suffered. You can find comfort and know-how in even the most cluttered past.

Your precious time is going to be guided by your values, so make sure they're clear. You can do this by claiming your happiest moments and fondest friends. Respect your hard-earned insights. But realize that other people may not see the world or their capacity to influence their own lives as you do. The method of survival you have chosen to handle challenges in your past can be fine-tuned to help you now.

Don't forget to take care of yourself while you are building on the past to make tomorrow brighter. To help you do that, here are five commandments that I wrote to help me take stock of my relationships while caring for my health:

MAINTAIN HONESTY OF COMMUNICATIONS

FIND JOY IN BEING AND BEFRIENDING

LEAVE OFF POSSESSING OTHERS

CLING TO VISIONS OF HOPE

GET ON WITH LIFE

SIX

STILL ALIVE:

Managing Your Medical, Social, and Economic Needs

My head was strapped in place, enclosed by a very unusual X-ray machine. My right arm was hooked to an IV pumping iodine dye mixture to my brain. The science fiction shapes of the ultra-modern CAT scan room gave off a weird effect. The laser beam rotated around my head until I was dizzy. Billy and the technician were on the other side of the futuristic wall. The CAT scan technician wore a sterile white uniform, looking from one monitor to another as she methodically pushed computer keys. Billy says it was as if she was looking at me from within my own head.

My mind was occupied with its own thoughts. Up to this point, my ill health had been relatively stable. These sudden and unexplainable symptoms brought home the reality of several very heavy biological possibilities. My conscious experience will ultimately be determined by some very basic, unconscious biological laws. I was discovering that living with dying involves

116

a lot more than my "hanging-in-there" mental attitude. Reciting Nietzsche's "That which does not kill me makes me stronger" doesn't always work. Yet, I was still alive.

Managing Your Medical Needs

In order to manage your illness over the months ahead, you will need to have a medical doctor in whom you have confidence. If you don't already have such a primary-care physician, start looking for one. If you do have a primary-care physician, you may still need a specialist. Ask friends or others you know with a similar problem to suggest a doctor.

There may be other resources for medical care available. Check to see if there is a toll-free hotline for people who have the same illness by calling 800-555-1212. Also, you may find a local social-service agency that can give you appropriate referrals. Yet another source for health care referral is your County Department of Health. In addition, health maintenance organizations (HMOs), if available to you, provide care for a monthly premium. HMOs tend to hold down costs, but will permit you to see only those physicians on their roster. There may be a local medical society in your area, which can provide a list of its doctor and hospital members. If you have a medical school nearby, you can check with them for a physician referral.

Make a list of what you feel are the important qualities and skills you want in a primary-care doctor, and go over it with each doctor you interview. You can make a list of the things you want to know about your health before you go.

Imagine just how you want the doctor's visit to go. Take time to think of ways to make the visit satisfying. Here are several things you may find important:

- Being provided with precise, comprehensive explanations of tests and treatments.

- Feeling comfortable with the office staff.

- Being satisfied with the doctor's style of giving advice.

- Receiving the quality of emotional support you feel comfortable with, especially regarding tests, examinations, and treatments.

It is important that you feel at ease talking with your doctor. This is a two-way street: Both of you have to be comfortable with the way you communicate. The doctor will be deciding if you are a person he or she wants to treat, as you are deciding if you want the doctor to treat you. You can't expect to have a doctor take whatever you want to dish out, but you can expect to participate actively in developing a working rapport.

I sometimes take a friend or care partner with me to help recall details, or to take notes for me. I ask the doctor before he begins the exam if my friend may stay in the room. Then my care partner or friend will help me to recall particular symptoms I might forget, or ask the doctor questions about some aspect of the routine care. I have my care partner help me put together a list of questions and information about my symptoms before I go for an appointment; in fact, we do this for one another. One doctor suggested I tape-record the instructions, if I wanted.

Your primary care doctor must be both willing and able to coordinate care among the specialists who treat his patients. Ask your doctor whom he usually refers his patients to for the specific problems you are likely to have. You can learn a lot about the physician's knowledge and resourcefulness by asking about the network of specialists he works with. If you have the opportunity to talk with other patients in his practice, ask them how good they consider their doctor. You might also consider asking your doctor how many cases he has treated that were similar to yours. Make sure you feel confident in your doctor.

Hanging in There author Spingarn cautions us: "Be scrupulous in checking out the credentials of those who offer you their services, whether they be as individual therapists or group leaders. This is not a time when you can afford to fall into the hands of poorly trained people who take advantage of your vulnerability." You may need to interview several physicians before you find one you are comfortable with.

If you want to check your M.D.'s credentials, you might look in the *Compendium of Certified Medical Specialists* (American Board of Medical Specialities). This annual publication will give you the doctor's age, medical school, date of certification, address of practice, and hospital where staff privileges are held. If your doctor has not been certified, ask, "Why not?"

Try to avoid making medical decisions as though there were two approaches to health care: traditional, like surgery, and nontraditional, like a macrobiotic diet. According to the Holistic Medical Association, holistic approaches to medicine emphasize personal responsibility for health, while including personal choices from both conventional treatments and nonconventional ones. The lesson we are quick to learn, being still alive, is that the quality in our daily living is better if we see our choices in terms of *both/and*, rather than in terms of *either/or*. For example, you might use both a vitamin treatment and an antibiotic treatment. Keep in mind that you are looking for a service that should be provided according to your needs and requirements.

Make an effort to learn how to be effective at controlling your symptoms. Don't be discouraged; even though you may not be able to totally control them, you can still learn how to treat and manage many of them. This is a chore that can be accomplished. You may need supportive care for various symptoms, like pain, mental function, gastrointestinal symptoms, skin problems, fever, weakness, and respiratory symptoms. Ask your doctor to help you with this by making a list of common symptoms and what to do about them. Be clear about how serious a symptom is, and do not delay seeking treatment. You might ask the doctor to code symptoms, like fevers and headaches, according to their urgency and treatment. This helps relieve some anxiety during periods of stability or remission.

I made a chart to help me with these health and illness issues that included:

Health Management Chart

Disease	Symptom	Treatment	Side Effects	Health Tips
AIDS	Candida	Acidophilus	None	Comply to a yeast-free diet, drink wheat grass juice.
AIDS	Fungal Nails	Soak nails in diluted Clorox	None	Don't garden without gloves
		Nizoral	Liver dysfunction	
AIDS	Fatigue	Free-form amino acids	None	Schedule activities with rest
		B-complex vitamins	None	stops.

Use the headings on my chart to make your own. Talk with your doctor about each symptom, asking how bothersome and serious each one is. You might want to list the options for treating each symptom in the Treatment and Side Effects columns before you decide which one or combination of more than one treatment you want to do. The suggested health tips should be effective at controlling symptoms, involving your active participation. The qualifications you have for items in your Health Tips column will reflect your overall strategy for coping with the daily hassles and crises. Your health tips may be the doctor's advice or based on your own past experience, from a book you have read, or another person's experience. Sometimes you'll have to make special time to take care of symptoms and sometimes you'll be able to work your medical self-care into your daily routine. But the tips should be aimed to make your life work well.

You will need to remain flexible to changing your tips for managing your health and illness. Chronically ill people are commonly seen trying to place themselves somewhere along a trajectory, seeking cues that suggest they are moving into a new phase, and waiting to define the next symptom as either temporary or a change in course. Each of us defines differently what we expect during the course and outcome of our illness.

Some words of caution are warranted here: Not all symptoms indicate a downward course. Some symptoms and bodily experiences may not be caused by your primary illness. Don't forget, symptoms that do occur as a result of your primary illness can often be effectively managed. Remember, too much emphasis on presenting symptoms can impair your desire and ability to actually manage them when they do occur. The approach I advise is one that avoids the pitfall of living a life filled with dread and dismay.

You will have to take time out to focus on nutrition and the basics of caring for yourself. Taking charge of your medical needs is essentially a task in learning how to satisfy powerful biological demands. Working through old relationships to reach new understandings is time-consuming, as are the other things mentioned. Adapting to the changes you will make in your personal relationships will take a lot of energy. When facing a life-threatening illness, diet takes on a lot more meaning than simply eating well.

Upon diagnosis, I began eating a balanced diet more regularly, one slightly higher in fiber content. I have gathered the information necessary to evaluate my diet, and have developed a diet that is supplemented by the appropriate and desired vitamins and minerals. I started by reading issues of *Prevention Magazine*. I focused my attention on articles about selenium ("Selenium, The Great Protector," by Debroa Tkac, *Prevention*, August 1983), vitamin E ("Vitamin E's New Frontiers of Healing," by Lewis Vaughn, *Prevention*, August 1983), beta carotene ("The Number One Anti-Cancer Vitamin," by Debora Tkac, *Prevention*, June 1983), vitamin C ("One Woman's War on Cancer," by Kerry Pechter, *Prevention*, August 1983), and the complex family of vitamin Bs ("Best Health Bets from the B Team," by Denise Foley, *Prevention*, April 1984). I read *The Cancer Prevention Diet*, by Michio Kushi (New York: St. Martin's Press, 1983), and learned how to balance my diet with nourishing whole foods. Then I got a book entitled *Megavitamin Treatment*, by Richard Passwater (New York: Simon and Schuster, 1976), which explained a safe way to take a lot of vitamins and minerals. This book helped me fight back with nutrition.

My primary-care physician has a record of my vitamin protocol, and I consult with him as I make changes in it.

I read Norman Cousins' book, *Anatomy of an Illness as Perceived by the Patient: Reflections of Healing and Regeneration* (New York: Bantam Books, 1979). This book helped me appreciate the personal power each person can claim to handle a life-threatening illness. In addition, the Cousins book helped me by teaching me how unconventional treatments, like laughter and vitamin C, can be used in conjunction with more conventional treatments.

You may benefit by developing a program of exercise that your doctor advises is safe, yet challenging. Try to spend at least one hour daily doing some type of exercise. Work within your physical limits. You may simply be stretching in the kitchen between tasks, and walking up stairs instead of taking an elevator. You may be lifting yourself up from bed. Physical exercise within our physical limitations is vital to our well-being. I enjoy the times when I feel good enough to roller-skate, jog, and play tennis. My studies in psychoneuroimmunology (PNI) have helped me understand how physical exertion causes chemical changes that can stimulate cells that fight disease. There are several ways that the mind can affect the body's defenses against disease. Sometimes I feel feverish and my muscles ache after I exercise more than usual. I understand from studies in psychoneuroimmunology that what I consider negative short-term effects of exercising, like rapid heart rate and feeling flushed, may actually be a enhanced short-term immune response that is positive in the long run.

Sometimes my regular schedule of physical exercise is interrupted by bouts with illness. Right after these episodes, it can be all too easy to push too much, causing a physical strain. Yet stop we must when our bodies tell us with a muscle cramp or a pain that we are pushing too hard. The question of titration, "How much do you take in order to gain the desired effect?", becomes the real question.

I have learned to strike a balance between over-exertion and being a "couch potato." I often feel less anxious and depressed when I am exercising than when I am not exercising. Still, suggesting to a friend that we sit in a cool place and simply visit produces its own comfort and joy. Physical exercise is a particular kind of stress on the body, and there are other kinds of stress and strain that are more negative.

Determining the level of stress you operate best under is essential to your quality of life. I enjoy yoga when I need to relax. Staying at the level of stress you function best at (titration to stress) is a critical balancing act when you have a life-threatening illness. You should select your own gauges or signs forewarning you of your threshold for stress; you probably already know what your stress signals are. The bottom line here is that your stress level be maintained at a point that is tolerable, to some extent manageable. By noticing your bodily reactions to stressful events, you can learn how to best limit your exposure to health-damaging high-stress levels. You can gauge your reactions to physical stress and take the time to relax from them.

Don't forget there are also positive aspects to stress. The first of these is that stress often indicates change, and change can be positive. In addition, it is important to acknowledge that some of us thrive on that aspect of stress that provides a challenge to our capabilities. In other words, some of us actually seek stress to relieve boredom. We create challenging deadlines for projects; we pack our schedules with social events without concern for a day of rest; and we set demanding goals in every aspect of our lives. Handling issues and events that are stressful gives us a feeling of being connected to the living world. The essential point to be summarized here is that we benefit by understanding both the kind and amount of stress with which we can thrive. This is the ecology of our time and space: We titrate to life.

I take the time to relax as needed each day and night. I usually play some soft music in the background, unplug the telephone, and lock the door. Then I get in a comfortable position and relax. Slowly, I begin taking deep breaths, relaxing further. I have several deep-breathing exercises I learned from a yoga class that help me calm down. I am able to control my fevers and several skin symptoms by relaxation. I believe I go still further with my imagery and self-suggestions to create well-being. I do not believe I can heal my car through autosuggestion, but I know I can influence my own health!

I have developed and refined my imagery techniques as these years since diagnosis have passed. I got started with visualization as an alternative treatment for cancer when I read *Getting Well Again*, which is reviewed in Further Reading. Then I applied the knowledge I had already acquired from reading several clinical method texts on relaxation methods. I relaxed with the beliefs I had grown to endorse from *The Way of Life According to Lao Tzu*, translated by Witter Bynner (New York: G. P. Putnam's Sons, 1944). When I felt I had harnessed the healing light, I imagined the light was my immune system's white blood cells, or lymphocytes. Then I focused on sending the light to attack my tumors.

I believe I am assisting my T-cells in achieving mature functioning. My understanding of cell-mediated immunity as those bodily reactions that specialize in fighting off viruses and attacking tumors enhances my imagery. I now combine my relaxation with self-statements that suggest that my immune system function better. My program begins with me fully relaxed and prepared to accept suggestions of healing and regeneration. I sometimes "grab" the first glimmer of white light that flashes in my mind's eye, holding the brilliant light like a still painting.

For the first three years since diagnosis, I took extract of bone marrow and thymus gland before imagery exercises. I understand that immune cells are born in the bone marrow, and that the thymus gland transforms newborn T-cells into mature T-cells. I spent time (1) envisioning my helper T-cells getting stronger in their aggressive assault to help other immune cells; (2) visualizing my suppressor T-cells lessening in number and getting out of the way of other immune cells; and (3) imagining my killer T-cells destroying cancerous and virus-infected cells, reminding them that they do remember and recognize what does and does not belong in my body.

When I visualize these effects, I also vocalize what I desire to happen. For example, I "talk to" the specific cells, instructing them as I move through what would typically take about two hours. I also speak angrily to the cancer cells, sometimes shouting at them to leave me—they do not belong and are not welcome. I believe that my own ecological system benefits from spelling out the congruence between my mental, vocal, visual, and physical expressions: Each of my senses is tapped to its fullest.

I have now simplified my imagery exercises, and also use a lot of positive thinking daily. After nearly five years of doing healing imagery, I relax, then use a mental command, like, *"Ready: Now!"* The simple cue *"Now!"* condenses months of working out the details of my healing imagery for cancer and AIDS. With one word, *"Now!"*, I command an orchestrated immune response. I have used biofeedback equipment to test the various prompts or cues that give me the most pleasure and comfort.

The feedback you get from your body is a kind of knowledge that deserves your attention and understanding. After all, while you are competent, decisions about your health care, social, and financial arrangements do rest with you. You may need details and definitions about the ethical and legal issues posed by a life-threatening illness, and if so, read the "President's Commission for the Study of Ethical Problems and Biobehavioral Research Report." This publication is available at your public library, or by writing to the President's Commission for the Study of Ethical Problems in Medicine and Biomedical and Behavioral Research, Suite 555, 2000 K Street, NW, Washington, D.C. 20006. This book contains official details and definitions about the ethical and legal issues posed by a life-threatening illness.

Managing your medical needs will involve a lot of coordination between specialists. Do yourself a favor and consider yourself a specialist on your physical experience. Take command of helping your body by spending the time and effort to exercise, eat well, and relax. Put the power of your positive thinking behind your physical healing!

Managing Your Social Needs

None of the friendships you have will be the same after your diagnosis. Some friends and family members will increase their degree of involvement in your life. You will notice who gets more involved and who doesn't. The changes in your medical status will impinge on every member of your social network. You may need help with basic care, like cooking and cleaning, changing sheets and taking temperatures. Equally important, you will need to have people who will step in and help you make the quality of your experiences worth the struggle of being alive. Sometimes the support you will need will be intimate conversation and sometimes it will be silent company, but having a primary-care partner or caring friend is a must!

Right after one partner in a couple receives a terminal diagnosis, the couple usually struggles to resolve their mixed emotions and make stronger commitments. At this time, both partners are apt to attribute their own and their spouse's behavior to the illness and its problems. You may not wish to have so much of your behavior attributed to your condition. For instance, you may want to rest at home because you need some time to meditate, not because you are handicapped by your illness. Overattributing events and behaviors to your illness can contribute to your feelings of being diminished as a person. *Don't let your illness take over your personality!*

My spouse and I needed to mourn the loss of our old life together before we could face a commitment to a new one. We did this by first comparing our old life together to the present one. Then we made adjustments to losses and rewards in each. We experienced the need to be clear about issues of care. I learned how to give direct statements of my need, intention, and limits. We sorted through feelings about each other and the illness. The abandonment and rejection we felt from others made our love stronger and our hearts closer. Our daily activities were changed, because I was somewhere between unemployed and self-employed. We have done many of the things we would have done before I became ill, but I have taken over more of the cooking and cleaning chores, as my illness permits. We have developed a new way of living, because we have faced each day with the attitude that we will make life as wonderful for each of us as possible.

A critical issue for you is that you not place those you care about in the unhappy position of trying to second-guess your feelings. If you are not clear about how you feel about your illness, or are trying to play down the impact of the stigma, you may not be very clear in communicating your views to your spouse. *Do not* keep your spouse in the dark about your needs because you are confused about them yourself. Attempt to express clearly that you're feeling mixed emotions.

If you are experiencing clear emotional or even physical needs, *do not* refrain out of pride from making them known to anyone, especially your spouse. Your illness may itself leave much leeway in the determination of how and when physical or emotional help is needed. Don't let your spouse or friend begin to feel inadequate because he or she can no longer predict what pleases you.

There are normal strains placed on relationships after one member has received a terminal diagnosis. Both people may feel pressured about the new roles that must be adopted. In addition, both can feel the strain of simply not knowing how to behave. You may find it difficult to argue as effectively as you did in pre-diagnosis days because the normal spouse or friend may be too "understanding." Whenever this happens, communicate your feelings to the person so as to re-normalize your communications.

Right after my own diagnosis, my partner began to do just about everything for me—cooking, cleaning, and shopping. Perhaps I would have enjoyed a geisha at some other time in my life, but at that time, being handled with "kid gloves" made me feel helpless and useless.

I was sitting at the table one afternoon when Bill approached me with a concerned look, asking, "Can I get you a glass of water?"

"Sure," I snapped, "and why don't you drink it for me while you're at it?" My point was received, and Bill turned to stomp away. I apologized for my remark, acknowledged his anger, and within a few minutes, we began talking about what kinds of assistance I felt comfortable with. I explained that I *wanted* to make him mad, because I was tired of always having things "my way." I needed a healthy amount of dialogue and some resistance to become as bold in facing my illness as I desired to be.

Your friends and family are apt to overestimate or

underestimate the degree to which you are physically or emotionally needy. Therefore, they may be prone to offering insufficient or excessive care. Your loved ones may be genuinely confused about the nature or seriousness of the new condition. Keep communications open and give accurate feedback to the people caring for you. Honest communications can solve a lot of these problems.

Your social needs may be in a state of flux as your illness causes different symptoms. You will need many of the social affiliations and contacts that you have always enjoyed. Some will no longer be physically possible, but many will be socially workable. Keep in mind that the opposite of social connectedness is social isolation, and that isolation has usually been considered a form of torture or punishment. If you are isolating yourself, you might consider talking with someone you trust about your feelings of social stigma.

If others are avoiding you and isolating you, consider the value of each particular person and act accordingly. In my experience, it has been healthful to close the door on some friendships. I do believe that relationships never end, though; they only change forms. So, as I realize who is friendly and supportive and who is not, I change my expectation more than I change my openness. Don't worry about eliminating harmful relationships, for what we are really doing is allowing nature to take its course. We are experiencing the time it normally takes friendships to run their course as remarkably compressed!

But don't forget that it can also be very rewarding

to work out the problems you have with another, and still have that person to call "friend." There have been many occasions when a strain between what I needed and expected was in sharp contrast to what was possible and available. When it comes to friends, it has helped me to keep in mind that: 'If a pint holds a pint, it's doing all it can!'

My friends encourage me to express my feelings about AIDS, and feel satisfied with the quality of my intimate experiences. It has helped me to make telephone contact with my friends frequently, especially if we can't visit. Having much contact with a network of supportive persons, I feel satisfied with the understanding I receive. The quality of problem-solving support that I have received from others has been particularly helpful. I also refuse help sometimes, when it doesn't feel very helpful.

The most positive kinds of social support include hugs and consistent displays of caring. The most powerful kind of social support comes from having someone to count on, someone who will love you through good times and bad. One way this support works is when it is harder to think of fun things because you are depressed: Ask for help in generating ideas about what to do from a friend. This kind of seeking social support has the dual effect of making you feel valued, and reminding you that you still have a pulse and walk among the living. In general, positive social support should make you feel that you are strong and capable enough to handle the illness.

Information about your illness can be a source of social support, but it may also be a source of social stigma. It may come from society through the media. Information is supportive when it contains helpful advice about how to adjust to your illness. On the other hand, it is negative and stigmatizing when it contains dramatic news of dreadful deaths due to a particular illness, and paints a picture of the victims as fitting certain negative stereotypes. Information is positive when it comes from well-informed family members, based on a hopeful attitude and medical fact.

A simple pat on the back from someone you love is powerful support. Love is a very strong form of social support. Here is a demonstration of the healing power of love. You'll need three things to do this exercise: a thermometer, a clock with a second hand, and some private time. Start by relaxing for a few minutes. Then check your pulse, locating it with your right index finger placed on your left wrist at the base of your left thumb; count the number of pulses in 15 seconds and multiply that number by 4. For example, if your pulse beats 20 times in 15 seconds, your pulse is 80 times per minute. Take your temperature. Make a note of these to refer to later. Next, imagine a time when you felt loved. Take care not to pick a relationship that has ended poorly, or one that is missed sorely. Alternatively, imagine that you truly love and accept yourself. Feel the calming effect of stroking your arms and shoulders. Don't make negative statements in your mind about yourself while you are doing this exercise. After fifteen minutes of this "love imagery," take your pulse and temperature and write it down.

Now, allow your mind to consume itself with thoughts of how another has angered you, or of how you may not like yourself. Dwell on the negative feeling of hate and self-anger for fifteen minutes. Recheck your pulse and temperature and compare your rates. Now, calm yourself back to normal. Make yourself a mental note about the person or event your angry mind brought forth for later consideration.

I have found that I have a lower temperature and pulse rate than normal when I am thinking "love." When I'm thinking anger and rejection, my fever goes up along with my pulse. Scientists have discovered other measures of biological and immunological changes that correspond to mood and thought. But the message here is the same: Thinking and feeling love can produce a calming effect. You can heal your body and your life, according to Louise Hay in *You Can Heal Your Life* (Santa Monica, California: Hay House, 1984), by pure love and self-acceptance.

Having the sense that it is okay to talk about our situation gives us support. It is supportive and socially constructive to express feelings about our illness. Sometimes, self-help groups provide the opportunity for ventilation of emotions, a process of "getting it all out." They have the advantage of allowing a friendship and caring bond to develop between group members and leaders that is not allowed in other types of counseling that require "professional distance." Sharing common experiences in a setting that encourages close-ness links us to social norms and common beliefs about our illness. You can learn how others interpret your illness. This kind of group experience helps one resolve what is appropriate and what isn't. Group experiences can help you uncover the social foundations of your attitudes, emotions, and hopes.

The people we walk among while we are still alive may have new and intense reactions to continuing our relationships. It is okay to acknowledge that the task of maintaining a wide range of casual interpersonal relationships may be too arduous and costly for you at this time. This strategy requires selecting a few positive social activities and friendships. You can de-crease stress in your life by reducing problematic, strainful interactions. Rely on social contact with a few people who handle their interactions smoothly and do not inflict high emotional costs on you. That strategy might be coupled with spending time alone, taking care of your health, and enjoying the day when these few loved ones are unavailable.

There are negative aspects of social support. These include the possibility that displays of affection and sympathy received from some people in your support network may wear thin over a long-term illness, turn-ing into irritation and resentment at your dependency. Members of the social-support network may provide slanted and incorrect information about your illness, prognosis, or treatment. Social attitudes about your particular illness may make others abandon you, or reject you with moral disdain. Some people will show an immediate burst of concern, but leave you coldly soon after.

I came to some conclusions about my most important social needs after I spent several weeks reliving the past while meeting the demands of the present. I need to feel loved. I concluded that the most important need I had was to be satisfied with the people who really care about me. I do need to have someone to depend on—and luckily do.

It's important that our social needs be taken care of. But this is not a one-way street; we ought to take time to make things a little easier for those friends and loved ones who give us their precious caring. Help your caring partner out by telling him or her how grateful you are for this love and support. Don't forget to ask your partner how he or she is feeling, too. Try not to demand too much time, and take care not to nag about every minor symptom. Make sure that your loved ones are getting the support they need by asking them what they need.

Managing Your Economic Needs

Taking care of your economic needs in the upcoming months will be an important task. You may have additional financial needs at a time when you have fewer resources. There may be a change in your ability to meet those needs. This situation requires a great deal of flexibility and tolerance. While you are still able, you will have to manage these new changes in your financial needs, but you don't have to do it alone. Your general well-being and satisfaction with life are influenced by how well you take care of your financial implications of your illness. Mundane financial chores, like paying rent and balancing accounts, take on a new urgency after a terminal diagnosis. You may need to get help with your budget.

Your health insurance is a very important aspect of your financial planning and management. If you do have health insurance, keep it and don't miss a payment! If you are leaving a job that provides you with group insurance or company-paid insurance, you will need to convert it. Read about how to convert your policy so you can keep it as an individual and follow each step. Look at your health insurance policy to see how much of the doctor's fees will be covered. How much of each hospital visit will be covered? Are prescription drugs covered, and if so, which ones? Are experimental treatments authorized? How is the billing handled?

If you don't have the savings to support yourself, you will need to find other sources for financial support. Your family may be able to help. Some friends will be able to help. You may need to call on your county welfare department initially, to get your needs met while applying for other monies. Consider asking a friend to help you through this financial management from the beginning.

It is tough to plan for medical expenses when you have a life-threatening illness if you can't predict the course of your illness very accurately. Nonetheless, try to get an idea of how much money you will need to manage your illness. If you are not working and your sick leave has expired, then you will need to scout out the sources available to you for disability income. Basically, there are four programs you may qualify for, including: your state's disability program, the federal Social Security Disability, the federal Supplementary Security Income programs, and your city's or county's welfare programs. Don't hesitate to ask a social worker or friend to take care of finding out what kind of disability payments you will qualify for; you may need some assistance with filling out forms and filing them.

I encourage you to take stock of your financial situation even before you think you need to. List your assets and your debts. Prepare a budget for the upcoming month. Then, based on what you need, start researching your options for financial support. Consider all the sources you can think of, including local churches, community groups, or social-service agencies in your area that will provide you with some basic needs, such as food, shelter, and clothing. Your housing situation may be altered by your illness. You may not be able to pay as much for housing now. You may have some special needs in your housing, like having your home nearby your hospital, or having a rail installed in your shower to hold on to. If you have lived

alone and still want to, work out the necessary arrangements for the assistance you may need. If you
rent, think about the consequences of telling your land-
lord about your illness. You may not want to open
yourself up to unnecessary risks for discrimination or
stigma from landlords or neighbors.

Managing your material needs will involve handling
the emotions your situation arouses in others. The
connection between love and money is not unfamiliar
to most of us. But in the illness situation, it can appear
in unique forms. Spouses are apt to give all they can,
and feel guilty when all they can give isn't enough to
meet your needs. Friends may feel imposed upon, or
hope that you will ask them for help. Family members
may assume you will let them "pick up the tab," or
they may not want to. When taking care of someone
who is ill involves providing for their financial needs,
it can become overwhelming. The fact that your needs
are so great may add to the strain on you.

Even though I do have some financial support, I still
have had difficulty paying my bills. I need more food
and medication than I can afford, and I do not have
someone to rely on for financial help. I have had to
turn for help to people I don't know, and some I really
don't like.

I have been aware of strange connections between love
and money before, but oddly, giving aid to the ill causes
a social strain between people. I have learned that giving
material support frightens some people. Giving financial
support to someone who is dying is a very special kind

of care-giving. The expectations and motivations of the person giving should be open for discussion between you. But be prepared—his fears of losing a loved one and of facing his own mortality may drive him away. Other people will simply not have much to give in the way of tangible assistance. Still others will not want you to *depend* on them. And a few will expect you to like them, cater to them, even bow to them.

I have experienced more than one incident that reminded me of my vulnerability and need. I have been forced to admit the limits of my self-reliance. I have had to remind myself a lot of times that I am not helpless, but I do need more help than I feel comfortable with. I have felt exasperated in such circumstances. My relief has come from reminders of myself when I was effective at managing tough times.

Managing your economic needs before your illness hinges on your employment. Yet there is more to being employed than financial reward. This part of working that is not material gain still has a place in your life after diagnosis: Working at something you are good at and that others value is satisfying and self-motivating. Your sense of "working" activity, of doing something that others value and require, and of joining with others similarly engaged at a particular time and place are important sources of meaning in life.

There are several legal considerations that you will have to make. It is important that you have a lawyer prepare a will and other necessary legal documents. A will can provide the people you care for with clear directions about how to treat your property. You can specify how your money and your personal property are to be distributed. You can specify if you want to be cremated or buried, and if you want a funeral or not. You'll need to find someone you trust to carry out the provisions of your will, an executor who will file your will in court. The executor will have to tend to a lot of financial details, like paying bills and dealing with insurance companies, so select someone you feel is competent at such matters.

In addition to your will, you may want to appoint a power of attorney. This document is intended to give another person the power to act in your capacity, to do every act that you may legally do through an attorney in fact. Another important legal document, called an authorization, permits the doctor to release information about your condition. The authorization is especially important to furnish information regarding your medical condition to those outside your biological family whom you want informed.

You may also want to protect yourself in the event that you develop problems requiring others to care for you totally; you can nominate a conservator of person and estate if a court finds it necessary to appoint a conservator. Check with your local library for books on estate planning for residents of your state, or ask a lawyer for help. A resourceful book is *Estate Planning for California Residents*, by Milton B. Scott (Chicago: Commercial Clearing House, Inc., 1983). This book helped me understand some of the considerations to make when planning for death and incapacity. I also found the book helpful because it gives good legal definitions and descriptions of what others may be required to do. Another useful book I discovered, *How to Avoid Lawyers*, by Don Biggs (Garland Press: New York, 1985), has a useful section on "Living Wills." States have specific guidelines and directives, often called a "Natural Death Act," that allow you to instruct your doctor not to use artificial methods to extend the natural process of dying. Before signing the directive, ask for advice from your physician and your lawyer. In most states, such a directive to physicians is valid for five years, and can be revoked by you at any time, even in the final stages of a life-threatening illness.

Learn what you can about the general management of your illness. The supportive care you may need to effectively manage your medical needs can even be socially gratifying. The bottom line about social support is that it lessens anxiety and facilitates active problem-solving. Managing your social needs will be more rewarding if you experience caring support that is both received and given. Managing financial matters after a terminal diagnosis must not be delayed. Make an effort to handle these practical material matters soon after your diagnosis. When deciding to forgo life-sustaining treatments, you need to make sure you understand the ethical, medical, and legal issues in treatment decisions. Dealing with these legal and financial matters is easier when you are not in the midst of a critical illness episode, so get your house in order now!

FURTHER READING

I have included this selection of references because reading about these things can help empower you as you cope with a terminal diagnosis. Some of the books I have included will be more useful to some than to others. I have described the special importance of each book in a way that will help you decide which ones to read, and which ones you might want others to read. These books helped me because they gave me information I needed to have, knowledge necessary to make solid decisions. I hope they will be useful for you, too.

Reading about your illness is probably the easiest thing you can do. Yet it will serve you in important ways. Reading and learning creates a mind-set, a stance, of being well-informed and involved. Reading about how other people have coped with various illnesses will encourage you to cope in your own ways. You can develop a sense of what others consider to be a "normal" reaction to life-threatening illness. You will develop a clear sense that you do have choices in your life. And the reading suggested here is by necessity only a partial list of the further reading you can benefit from. Many of the books I have included in this section have reference and resource information that will lead you to additional reading.

Carroll, David. *Living with Dying*. New York: McGraw-Hill Book Company, 1985.

This book is highly recommended for those coping with the death of a loved one. *Living with Dying* is a guide to open and honest discussions on topics that include: Sex and the dying person, suicide, dealing with difficult or dishonest doctors, "pulling the plug" on artificial life support, planning funeral arrangements, grieving, speaking about death to children, and negative feelings of the family toward the dying patient. This book offers the family and friends of the dying person much useful information.

Feigenberg, Loma. *Terminal Care Friendship Contracts*. New York: Brunner/Mazel Publishers, 1980.

In this book, Feigenberg focuses on the cancer patient and his or her relationship to loved ones and care providers. The aim of *Contracts* is primarily to present a special method for psychological terminal care. This book is a significant contribution to social psychology and psychodynamic psychiatry.

Hutschnecker, Arnold A. *The Will to Live*. Englewood Cliffs, New Jersey: Prentice-Hall, 1951.

Psychosomaticist Dr. Arnold Hutschnecker writes of the power of hope among ill patients. He explains that most people maintain at least a little hope. Those without hope have the attitude that there is no end to their suffering. Those with hope have confidence in the desirability of survival. Drawing on the theme of man against himself, he discusses the legion of the tired and the destructive drives. The emotional dynamics of illness are discussed in a readable way that offers advice of how not to shorten life and how to cultivate the will to live.

Kübler-Ross, Elisabeth. *On Death and Dying*. New York: Macmillan, 1969.

This book is probably the contemporary classic work in the study of death and dying. *On Death and Dying* aims to help the reader establish an intellectual understanding of the stages of dying. A major problem this work has faced is the misunderstood notion that there are distinct developmental stages of emotional/psychological reactions to terminal illness. Actually, *On Death and Dying* is a very frank and helpful guide to information about feelings during the dying process. The model of psychological defenses described include denial/isolation, anger, bargaining, depression, and acceptance. Kübler-Ross has conducted in-depth interviews with chronically ill, hospitalized patients at various stages of their illness and was able to show how and what feelings they experience. In contrast to commonly held views about the work of Kübler-Ross, she has seen and reported cases in which so-called phases are not sequential. For example, denial and acceptance of illness and mortality exist simultaneously.

Martelli, Leonard J. *When Someone You Know Has AIDS*. New York: Crown Publishers, Inc., 1987.

The author of this book is a writer and AIDS "care partner." To write *When Someone You Know Has AIDS*, Martelli interviewed hundreds of friends and relatives of people with AIDS and collaborated with therapists Fran D. Peltz and William Messina. The result of Martelli's efforts is a writing style that captures the horror and the rage that people with AIDS experience. Compassionate and informative, *When Someone You Know Has AIDS* is a book especially useful to anyone who cares about a friend, relative, or lover with AIDS or ARC (AIDS-related complex).

The concept of "care partner" is used extensively throughout the book to mean a caring friend. There are a lot of things about being a care partner that are special; as Martelli says:

> Soon you may wonder, "What is happening to me?" "Why do so many of my conversations seem silly to me?" "Why is my job less interesting?" "Why am I always so restless?" "Why do I always seem to want to leave where I am to go somewhere else, usually to where my friend with AIDS is just then?" You will have become a carepartner,

a caring friend. You will have begun to live a life probably more intense and painful than anything you knew before, but a life certainly richer and more rewarding.

When Someone You Know Has AIDS contains clear explanations of the special concerns of care partners and friends to people with AIDS. It helped me to better understand what the people around me were going through, providing some solutions to offer them for problems generated by my illness and others' reactions to my illness. The chapters on the medical aspects of AIDS give concise descriptions of the illness, its symptoms, and the experimental drugs and programs used to deal with AIDS. Topics covered in other chapters include coping with the emotional aspects of diagnosis, dealing with financial matters, forms of intimacy, and conquering grief and loss. The focus of these discussions and personal stories is to help anyone who cares about someone with AIDS. Yet the book is written in a way that appeals to the shared experience of mortality. Martelli leads the reader to a common ground of caring and provides them with the information they will need to care effectively.

If you are interested in the topic of AIDS, another book that is helpful especially to parents is *When Someone You Love Has AIDS* (BettyClare Moffatt, Santa Monica, California: IBS Press, 1986), written by a mother of a person with AIDS.

Passwater, Richard A. **Supernutrition**. New York: Pocket Books, 1976.

This is a reasonable manual to super-nutrition through taking megavitamins. I found the "Supernutrition Curve" most useful in determining the amount of vitamins needed to produce beneficial, rather than detrimental, effects. The author is stern about the lack of educational requirements for physicians in the area of nutrition, insisting that the two-state theory of "The person is either sick or well," is not correct, and runs against common sense, with health having many more than two gradations. He argues against a mere placebo effect for vitamins. Human beings need more nutrition than is available through our modern diet, Passwater argues, because man suffers from unnatural factors such as carcinogens and other chemical pollutants, and has been removed from natural environments. In addition, modern man is deficient in vitamin C as well as other vitamins. This book is a good guide to developing your own super-nutrition plan, whether it be for cancer or heart disease, or for staying young longer.

Pendleton, Winston K. **Handbook of Inspirational and Motivational Stories, Anecdotes and Humor**. New York: Parker Publishing Company, 1982.

The author of this handbook boasts that "opening the pages of this handbook is like stepping into a public speaker's department store. Here you will find everything under one roof." What the author has done is to select some of the quotations and bits of humor from notes and papers he has collected for over thirty years. In this book, you can select from among more than six hundred categories to find a quote, anecdote, or joke. You can use this book to help both yourself and others. While you may need to deliver some speeches only to yourself, some can be made more meaningful to others by using this book.

Robertson, John. *The Rights of the Critically Ill.* New York: Bantam Books, 1983.

This book is recommended as an excellent guide to the legal rights of the critically ill. It contains comprehensive information on laws by citing legal decisions made in state and federal courts. The principal purpose of this ACLU handbook is to inform individuals of their legal rights. *The Rights of the Critically Ill* is written from the patient's perspective. I found it useful in making several important decisions, as the book focuses on making life and death decisions under intense stress and overwhelming emotion. Some of the questions addressed include: "Do cancer patients have the right to know the truth about their condition?" "Do family members have any rights to know the truth?" "If a patient is not conscious, who makes the decisions?" "Can a person refuse medical treatment that would keep him alive?" "Does a critically ill person have a right to commit suicide?"

Shepard, Martin. ***Someone You Love Is Dying: A Guide for Helping and Caring***. New York: Crown Publishers, 1975.

After a successful background that included medical school, a general internship, and fourteen years of psychiatric training and practice, the author already had had ample opportunity to attend the dying and later on to hear tales told by the bereaved. Yet this book was prompted by the author's personal experiences of living out his father's dying with him. He shows how the living can learn from the dying. Shepard gives ample discussion to the "Why Me?" question, and issues of medical disclosure of information. This book is especially meant to teach those persons who have a dying loved one. It is intended as a professional tool, and has a lot of technical style, but it shows how professionals get personal when death hits close to home. In addition, the book includes important details about dying at home. This book also presents coping strategies for the experience of bereavement.

Simonton, Carl O., Matthews-Simonton, Stephanie, and Creighton, James L. ***Getting Well Again***. New York: Bantam Books, 1978.

This work reviews research on the interrelationship of the mind, the body, and the disease processes. *Getting Well Again* outlines treatment methods developed by the authors and discusses these methods with direct applications in combating cancer. *Getting Well Again* encourages the patient to take active part in changing feelings of hopelessness and depression. The authors encourage taking responsibility for being well, facing the fears of living, as well as the fears of dying. Relaxation techniques play an important role in producing the desired effect of the treatments they design. Their procedures of visualization to combat cancer have been sharply criticized by some, while others applaud them. I have found the book helpful in learning new ways to look at my illness and to cope with getting well again. The basic approach of the book helps me to see each illness episode as including the task of getting well.

A more recent publication that does a fine job of advancing many of the ideas put forth by the Simontons is *Love, Medicine and Miracles* by Bernie S. Siegel, M.D. (New York: Harper & Row Publishers, 1986).

Spingarn, Natalie D. ***Hanging in There: Living Well on Borrowed Time.*** New York: Stein and Day, 1983.

I recommend *Hanging in There* for any person facing a life-threatening illness. The book favors traditional medical approaches, but it has a lot to offer people who have been told by a medical authority that they will die soon. This book describes the process of transforming what was formerly considered a sentence of death into an opportunity for intense appreciation of life. Living with a serious illness herself, the author articulates her own dealing with the medical and nonmedical aspects of having a life-threatening cancer. Spingarn has solid advice for women who have experienced a mastectomy; she also offers her analysis of the Simontons' work on cancer (see *Getting Well Again* by C. O. Simonton, et al.), arguing that the relationship between stress and cancer does not hold up. "Common sense tells me that many people I know who are not depressed at all, including innocent children, develop ugly cancers; conversely, many depressed, seemingly helpless, hopeless people go about their business, cancer-free. Common sense tells me that my perky, barking Corgi dog Patrick died sadly and suddenly of lung cancer last winter, and he did not even smoke, much less suffer depression."

Weisman, Avery D. *On Dying and Denying: A Psychiatric Study of Terminality.* New York: Behavioral Publications, Inc., 1972.

The author's primary goal in writing this book was to understand more about the reality of death and to find the practical significance of mortality. He believes that we must stand firm and face the ghosts of our fears. He directed a project on death and denial that interviewed over 350 patients during 1962–1965; these were cancer patients, aged people suffering from different illnesses and degrees of senescence, myocardial-infarction patients, pre- and postoperative patients believed to be terminal, and psychiatric patients who were conspicuously preoccupied with death. Conquering fears of death permits people to occupy themselves with living. The book contains important contributions to understanding physical, mental, and emotional experiences of terminality for professional health care workers.

EPILOGUE

Even though your medical prognosis may be grim, you can persist in facing it. In reading this book, you have hopefully gained some tips on how to manage your reaction to diagnosis. You know how others may treat you if they know of your illness. You can handle coping with daily living in a way that enhances your health and morale. You know about hope, and planning for the ones you love. You know what kind of working through of relationships and past events will pay off in the most positive ways. And, you are still alive, handling your medical, social, and material needs.

The changes in your personal and social relationships that are brought on by your illness will take a lot of getting comfortable with. And you may feel that when you do get accustomed to living with one new symptom, another springs up that requires more changes in your life. Your flexibility in managing both medical symptoms and personal relationships is the key to adapting.

Act on behalf of your own welfare! Starting with the ideas in this book, you can build your own personal guide to coping with your life-threatening situation. Persevere in maintaining the health-promoting regi-

Epilogue

men you select. Hold steadfastly to your desires for quality living, despite the obstacles. You have made it this far. You are still alive. You can climb the mountain of troubles ahead, and cherish a few flowers along the way. But, you must believe you can!

Like the "Little Engine Who Could," you must keep repeating the words:

"I think I can . . ."